The Basis of Organization

Cells, Humans and Multi-Humans

The Basis of Organization: Cells, Humans and Multi-Humans

Pranab Majumder

Durham, NC

The Basis of Organization © 2016-2020 by Pranab Majumder.

Pranab.Majumder@gmail.com

Published at Durham, NC
First Edition (a): 2020

Edited and prepared in LyX

Proofreading: Chris Huebner

Cover illustration: Pranab Majumder
Cover includes graphics created in: QuickMan
(https://sourceforge.net/projects/quickman/)

Library of Congress Cataloging-in-Publication data

Majumder, Pranab, 1968-

The Basis of Organization: Cells, Humans and Multi-Humans/ Pranab Majumder

p. cm.

Includes Index

Paperback ISBN 978-1-7357796-0-7

Ebook ISBN 978-1-7357796-1-4

Large Print Paperback ISBN 978-1-7357796-2-1

1. Business-Strategy. 2. Philosophy-Metaphysics-Structure. I. Majumder, Pranab. 1968-.

II. Title.

Classification: LCC HD30.19 | DDC: 658.001, 117

LC Control Number: 2020917794

Dedicated to Never Completely Belonging

Contents

Acknowledgments

I want to thank many friends who have read earlier versions of these words, from when it was merely a short version of the appendix, to its still-evolving present form.

Rudra Dutta, my high school friend, and Madhulavi, my wife, were the victims of many versions, from the very first one. We are co-conspirators on many other hobbies, and I imposed on them to read that first bare skeleton, consisting of rather cryptic sentences. Madhulavi also suggested constructing the map that is shown in the first few chapters.

Anupam Agrawal, with whom I overlapped at two schools as a student, was meticulous in providing me detailed feedback on a long version of the manuscript. His encouragement gave me hope that perhaps one more person beyond me can understand these words.

Chris Huebner, during his time as a student at Duke University, was kind enough to proofread this manuscript very carefully-catching errors, unexplained tangential thoughts and jarring style changes that accumulated over the many days (years) it took me to put these words together.

In addition, many friends at work, in the local community and other networks had to patiently listen to my attempts to explain everything in the universe according to the principles of this framework- Kaushik Sen, James Emery, Nikhil Banerjee, Siddhartha Mitra, Jane Smith and others. Thank you for your patience.

If you are reading these words, I thank you too. I apologize in advance for any sections that are difficult to understand- I will continue to try to make them clearer. If very few people read these words, I thank you, the rare reader, even more.

Foreword

After working as a professor for about four years, I got some good news. My research paper (with co-authors, of course) had been accepted to a prestigious journal of our field. I knew that if I could repeat this process a few times then I would have a great shot at tenure. Tenure, for the uninitiated, is a mark of my acceptance into the small club of my peers, in addition to bringing job security.

However, what should have been an occasion for celebration ended up depressing me. For four years we had toiled over the mathematical model presented in the paper, transforming it from a readable document into something that many of my peers would find intriguing precisely because they could not fully understand it on the first read.

As a business school academic I had hoped that my research would make a difference in how businesses operate. Yet that seemed increasingly unlikely. My research was far removed from having any immediate impact, and I failed to perceive much value in what I did (beyond the obvious benefit of keeping my job). I estimated that each of my papers would be read by less than five people, and that was extremely frustrating for me.

I wanted my research to be meaningful for business practice, and I wanted to see it happen in a reasonable time frame. I wanted my research to be "real." During an introspective period I found myself asking this question "What is real in all that I do as a researcher?" The answers I came up with led only to frustration.

A couple of years into this constant search for "realness", one morning I happened to be watching the 2008 Olympic Games.

That is when it hit me like a truck. There is nothing real in most of what we humans do. The resulting conceptual destruction was just as extensive- it indicated to me that I may have been chasing the wrong measures of what is real, or what makes an impact.

The Olympic Games is a multi-billion dollar spectacle and is the culmination of lifetimes worth of effort from athletes, coaches and countries. It is watched by hundreds of millions of humans all over the world. Yet, at the end of it, what is the "real" benefit of running a hundred meters faster than all others by a hundredth of a second? Where in modern life (outside such games) will running this fast help you find more food, shelter or other "real" rewards? Yet here we were, watching the worldwide broadcast, with some quite material benefits coming to the winner of the 100 meter dash (and some momentary prestige to the host country).

Similar constructed "competitions" abound- look no further than your country's collegiate and professional sports leagues and various televised singing and dancing competitions. However, the social benefits of non-functional competitions are also quite real- Olympic gold medalists get recognition and sponsorship, and professional league players can sign endorsements for millions. So, what is more important- the "real" competitions for food and shelter, or these arbitrarily constructed ones? And why?

For the past fourteen years I have chased the threads of this original question, and this book represents its evolving answer. I set out to write a simple explanation of the world as I see it. Long-suffering family and friends assure me quite clearly that my explanation is not that simple. My apologies for this shortcoming.

There are other shortcomings too. First, this is a work-in-progress. Many ideas here have to be refined from their current clunky forms. Second, my answers are colored by my own interest in the natural sciences of physics, chemistry, biology and similar topics, as well as my professional interest in business operations and strategy. Finally, my knowledge of these and other areas, and the examples I provide, are incomplete and often incorrect. Please help me correct them, and bring them up to the current state of knowledge.

The impreciseness of my initial attempts forced me to restructure these thoughts. This restructuring first led to a rational framework, and then to discussions about the implications and insights from that framework. Part I presents the framework, with discussions to flesh it out, and Part II presents some applications. The rational framework itself is presented in an appendix.

There is another way to see this work that may explain where it lies in the continuum of human knowledge. One popular critique of research (and professors) is that professors are people who strive to learn more and more (through research) about less and less (more narrow topics) until they know almost everything about almost nothing. In that spirit, this work attempts to explain less and less (using more abstractions) about more and more (all areas of knowledge) until it claims to know almost nothing about almost everything. It is probably just as useful (or useless) to the average person in their daily lives.

This is also an opportunity for you to apply your own interests to this project. If you wish, you can use this framework to understand the context that you work in- whether that is in a large corporation, or in your community. I hope this will help you figure out how to channel your efforts towards the most worthy personal or social goal.

Finally, I don't think that any of the parts of the following framework are new- at best, all we can claim is that they may have never been put together in this particular form.

Pranab Majumder
Durham, NC
9th September, 2020.

Part I

The Basics

Chapter 1

Preface to The Basics

Introduction

"Why is the world organized this way?" This is the single question we will attempt to answer. It has an ongoing and evolving answer. The world continues to organize itself in different manners, while also decaying and breaking down in other ways. It is a dynamic system that we can study in parts, and perhaps try to look forward to see where it is going. Ultimately, our curiosity relates to our role in this scheme of things.

We have always been curious about how the world works and how it is organized, and we have been gathering knowledge and observations from even before we were modern humans. Ten thousand years ago all of mankind's knowledge could be contained in the mind of one person. It was lost almost as fast as it was created. There were very few mechanisms to transfer the learning from generation to generation, or from one village settlement to another in the face of frequent migrations and disruptions. With the advent of writing, printing, scientific inquiry, libraries, societies and other modern mechanisms our store of knowledge has been growing larger, and at an ever faster pace. In the late nineteenth century one person could hope to learn all scientific knowledge (that is physics, chemistry, biology and related fields) in their lifetime. Today, that is impossible. Now we gather copious amounts of trivial data, and also continue to add to knowledge at a fierce pace with the aid of information gathering and processing technologies.

Thus it is natural that in academia each of us specializes in the field of our choice. We participate in learning from and contributing to knowledge in these fields. We are specialized into tribes of scientists, researchers, practitioners, empiricists, consultants and administrators in these fields. Every once in a while one of us wanders over to another area, and out of these collaborations many new and interesting sub-fields are created. With the current state of our brains and our interaction with stores of knowledge, this is perhaps all that we can hope for.

There is still, in all this detail, some place for those of us who wish to integrate all these fields of knowledge into common frameworks, rather than subdivide and specialize into increasingly detailed inquiries. All this effort to gather details has the potential to answer any specific question we can ask. The irony is that it also makes the task of integrating all this knowledge into one overarching framework appear much more daunting.

About this Attempt

We will attempt to present a framework that will explain the organization of the world around us. We do this using a single set of rules that can be applied to multiple contexts, from atoms and molecules, to cells and living beings, all the way to humans and organizations. We will also present the basic mechanism of organization that creates a more complex context from simpler contexts. For example, molecules are created from atoms, cells are created from molecules, and hives are created from insects.

The same set of rules cannot sit comfortably across such vastly different situations. Please suspend disbelief at the obvious fallacies of this attempt so that we can find out together what can be gained from viewing the world at this extreme level of abstraction. Is there something about the manner in which cells organize into clusters that can be applied to how wolves form a pack, or perhaps how firms create an industry group? Is there something about how bees form a hive that can provide insight into proto-life a few billions years ago on Earth? That is the prize at the end of this road.

We are not there yet. We have some concepts and terms that seem to work for three or four of the contexts, but become meaningless when we go down to the earlier contexts, or become too simple for the complexity of the later contexts. Some of the terms we use may have analogous agencies in other contexts, but it is quite a stretch thinking of them as similar concepts. Nevertheless, what we have so far gives us hope that we should try to come up with parallel concepts that are applicable to other (maybe even to all known) contexts. Some of this framework may allow us to understand a few contexts in a much more holistic manner.

When I first stumbled upon these concepts my first reaction was to look at as many contexts as I could in order to find confirmation and support. That is not the way of inquiry.

Inquiry makes a concept stronger by trying to disprove it, not by trying to prove it. The process of science is driven towards testing facts. There is no corresponding process to check frameworks. A framework can often continue to exist as long as a set of internally consistent set of concepts supports each other. The mere rejection of a fact here and there does not cause a framework to collapse.

One way to test the validity of frameworks is to undertake the painful process of reducing a framework to its basic axiomatic truths, the ones which are the foundation of all else that forms the framework. If these basic axioms are flawed, then the rest of the structure has no hope. If these basic axioms are valid, the framework starts from a structurally sound basis, but there is still a lot of work to be done.

What we are proposing here is a framework, which we are trying to make internally consistent while trying to explain as much of the external world as we can. We have presented it in a manner where it should be clear what the foundation for each claim is, and in a manner where the foundation itself is concise enough to understand.

How to use this Book

We depend upon you to help take this framework forward. This is in no form a complete book. There will probably be many conceptual errors and inappropriate examples. We can only hope that this framework is improved marginally each time we attempt to apply it to a different field of knowledge. With each attempt we will be forced to tweak the framework so that it applies better to the new context without becoming completely invalid for the other contexts.

What is your area of expertise? Please use this book as a workbook, and we will be delighted to hear back from you about your experience in applying this framework to your area. I grew up loving biology, physics and chemistry (up to about a college freshman level), and then spent most of my time on the business side of the world, of which I understand only a small part. We need your perspective to make this framework better.

This is a call for collaboration, not a presentation of a completed work. Let us start our quest.

Caveats

We claim none of these following individual thoughts as original. The fact that we have been able to come up with them also means that they can be inferred or derived by many others. Every thought that we put down here has been observed by natural philosophers and scientists over the centuries. They must have also been inferred by many more whose words were lost, and also by those who focused on action rather than words. To all of them, as well, our homage.

This is our attempt to capture the current state of our thoughts. Since the process of writing itself crystallizes a number of thoughts, it is certain that by the time we reach the end of this attempt, many of the thoughts we wrote down in the earlier stages will look weak and dated. Nevertheless, we will put them down.

Warnings

We will discuss many evil things and many things which are morally reprehensible. All of us are creatures of the social order, and hold many values dearly. We are willing to fight for them and go to war, or send our kids into battle to defend these values.

Please withhold moral judgments on everything that we discuss here, no matter how obvious such judgment may appear. This is no mere trigger warning- we may discuss and deconstruct any human institution, and may attempt to point out the arbitrariness of many self-evident truths. We must aim to understand the world, as it is, to the best of our abilities, before we can chart a path towards making it as we want it to be.

Why?

Disruption is everywhere in the human world. How will these disruptions play out, and what will the structure of the new order that emerges next look like? Over these early years of the twenty-first century (this is 2019 now) increased communication, transportation and information processing technologies are brutally destroying many of the institutions and organizations we have grown up in and take for granted.

Perhaps every generation looks at the recent past and is amazed at the change they have seen. We are uncertain what the nature of social interaction, education, work and play will be in a decade or two from now, and what our roles will be in it. We hope that this framework may help add to our understanding of how these technological and social disruptions will play out.

On a personal note, I am one of the most risk-averse individuals I know. My entire life depends upon being a good citizen of a well-structured and moral human society. I am occasionally revolted by some of what the rest of this framework seems to imply. But I must present it as I see it simply because the weight of evidence from other parts of the universe tell me that it is so.

Chapter 2

Questions, Layers, and a Map

2.1 Questions

Consider the following strategic questions[1]:

- Why do we have to compete all the time?

- Why do we have disease, old age and death?

- Why can't we eliminate all thieves and cheats?

- Why can't the government regulate all large corporate activities?

- Why do large companies in the US have free speech?

- What is the difference between the business environments under capitalism and communism circa 1950?

- Why do we spend so much on war machines when there is so much hunger and poverty?

---

[1]Since this is a book about strategy, we have not chosen equally relevant questions from physics, chemistry, biology, sociology, genetics, anthropology or any other field.

- Why does 1% of the population control a large fraction of the world's assets?

Each of these questions has an analogy in biology, chemistry, sociology, business, politics and other fields.

For example, consider "thieves and cheats". The thieves and cheats in biology are the various animals and plants that steal from or kill other plants and animals, both unicellular and multicellular. In business they are the organizations that hunt and dismember other organizations. In politics they may be the opportunists who claim to represent their constituents, but are motivated primarily by personal profit.

Similar questions have sent humans on life-long quests. This had led to the creation of mass movements, religions, and some very successful businesses.

You too must have many questions in your mind similar to the questions listed above, perhaps based on your field of expertise. You may also have memories of things and incidents which stuck in your mind because they did not "fit" with already-established answers. Please collect them, and write them down. Perhaps we will be able to answer the more abstract and strategic forms of your questions during the course of this book.

2.2 Our Objective

Our objective is to come up with a set of definitions and processes that are general enough to be applied to any given context so that when we work our way through each example, it will show the path to the next context. In this manner we will construct the world as we see it.

2.3 Layers

As we have learned from the combined efforts of individuals in different fields, the world is organized in layers. Each of these layers is a fascinating and deep field(s) of study, and the study of any one layer can occupy the lifetimes of many researchers and thinkers.

Let us start by listing out these layers. The boundaries between layers is an arbitrary choice made to facilitate the discussion[2].

The layers are:

- Quantum Physics: The first layer is deep inside Quantum Physics. I know nothing more about this than what I have read in popular articles on the nature of the first few microseconds of the Big Bang. Are there any layers before that? There must be. Shall we ever find them all out? We don't know, but we should keep on searching.

- Subatomic and Atomic Physics: The next layers are probably Subatomic and Atomic Physics. There seems to be some consensus among physicists about the nature of these layers, although to say that this layer is weird is an understatement. In this layer there are entities that are both solid and nebulous at the same time. There is an ocean of froth from which all subatomic and atomic particles arise. There are opposite types of entities in this froth which keep canceling each other uncountable times. In fact, when we slow folks actually "see" an atom, it is only what survives as a remainder at the end of these battles. The atom we see is not even the same one from one moment to another, being replaced by an identical twin every time.

- Inorganic and Organic Chemistry: Once we get into the next layer of molecules, we are in the two fields of Inorganic Chemistry and Organic Chemistry. Inorganic chemistry deals with simpler molecules, while organic chemistry deals with longer molecules and molecules that replicate under certain conditions. Both of these subjects contain vast areas of knowledge that researchers have tried to uncover

---

[2]There are many curiosities that sit squarely at the boundaries- we have mentioned a few of them in different places in this book. These are equally fascinating pieces of the puzzle.

since the early days of alchemy. Our knowledge is still rather limited in scope since there are many molecules to study throughout the universe, and scientists are restricted to study what we deal with most of the time here on earth[3].

- Viroids and Viruses: The next layer consists of what we know about pre-life, which is the area of Viroids and Viruses. To argue whether viroids existed before there were any cells to infect is a strange conjecture. Thus, if there is no higher layer available in the environment, viroids are inorganic in their chemical behavior. But in the presence of living cells they "come alive" in some sense. Go figure.

- Single Cells: Moving up another layer in biology we come to single cellular creatures and perhaps ad-hoc multi-cellular organisms like slime molds. These creatures have a wealth of organization, structure and function within themselves, utilizing chemistry to beautiful purpose. There is a great diversity in the details of single-cells- their environments, shapes, activities and every other aspect of living. They use a variety of energy sources, from capturing sunlight to capturing the energy from sulfur compounds in deep sea volcanic vents.

- Multi-Cellular Organisms: The next layer is multi-cellular organisms, some of which are more exclusive than others. There are jellyfish which allow the stinging cells of their prey to migrate to their own tentacles (instead of being dismembered during digestion). Our own bodies are multi-cellular organisms that have identical copies of one set of DNA (allowing for subsequent mutation), which still have to work with a large number and variety of single-celled bacteria to complete activities as basic as digesting food.

---

[3]When we get serious about living on the other planets in our current carbon-based forms, our knowledge will have to increase by an order of magnitude. If we become able to recreate the human form on the basis of other types of atoms or with a different chemistry, then the subject will become seriously interesting.

- Hives and Packs: The next layer consists of hive organizations which feature collections of multi-cellular organisms, each of which can only survive short periods without other members. Examples of these are hives of ants and bees, and to some extent packs and herds of animals. Thus, the individual insects and animals have a limited degree of autonomy, and a degree of flexibility in their tasks and specialization.

- Sociology and Anthropology: As the complexity of the individual multi-cellular organism increases, the hive organization is replaced with a social organization. The degree and complexity of interaction between members changes from simple chemical signaling to more complex modes of signaling. This includes expressions, gestures, language and writing. In extreme cases the social organization can also be a cult, where all members think alike and are conditioned to reject thoughts that challenge a self-reinforcing framework of concepts as the basis of the cult's structure.

- Mega-Organization: Finally there are the mega organizations of multi-cellular organisms- religions, countries, companies and economic systems. They encompass whole new areas of knowledge as well: Religion, Politics, Economics and Business.

It may seem that there is no end to the details that we can uncover, and no end to our learning about the nature of our universe. A century ago we passed that point when one human could hope to learn all the current scientific knowledge in one lifetime. In recent years we have seen an explosion in the amount of information captured by precise devices that threatens to overwhelm those asking even the most basic questions.

We embark on this quest because we believe that there is an essential set of principles that drives the universe to cause new layers to emerge on top of previous layers. It is not always certain that a new layer will emerge, since it is a delicate process. It can take a long time, with many dead ends. When one such layer finally emerges it quickly (relatively speaking) establishes a new order so that, in retrospect, it seems inevitable that it should have eventually existed.

2.4   The Map

The map in figure 2.1 is how we will attempt to present the framework in Part I. The framework is used to show a path from one layer to another. We start from entities in one layer, and through an appreciation of their context and motivations arrive at entities in the next layer. Thus, we complete the full circle to come to a place similar to that we started from, but one layer more complex.

So, here is the basic description of the map.

- Chapter 2: Start with a layer as described in this chapter.

- Chapter 3: Entities, or distinct beings exist in each layer. Entities are mortal- they are born, and they die. If any of them do not wish to survive, they are free to do so.

- Competition for resources takes place among the entities which wish to survive.

- A strategy is the primary differentiation between competing entities. A strategy may not be unique to the entity, and may be context dependent.

- Long-term survival is the goal of all strategy.

- Chapter 4: Uncertainty makes the goal of survival difficult. Uncertainty can lead to death due to injury or starvation.

- The largest source of uncertainty for any entity is the actions of other entities most similar to it.

- Going alone means that the entity gets larger rewards less frequently and faces the risk of death from starvation or injury. Collaborating with others means that the entity gets a share from all rewards any member of the group gets. This

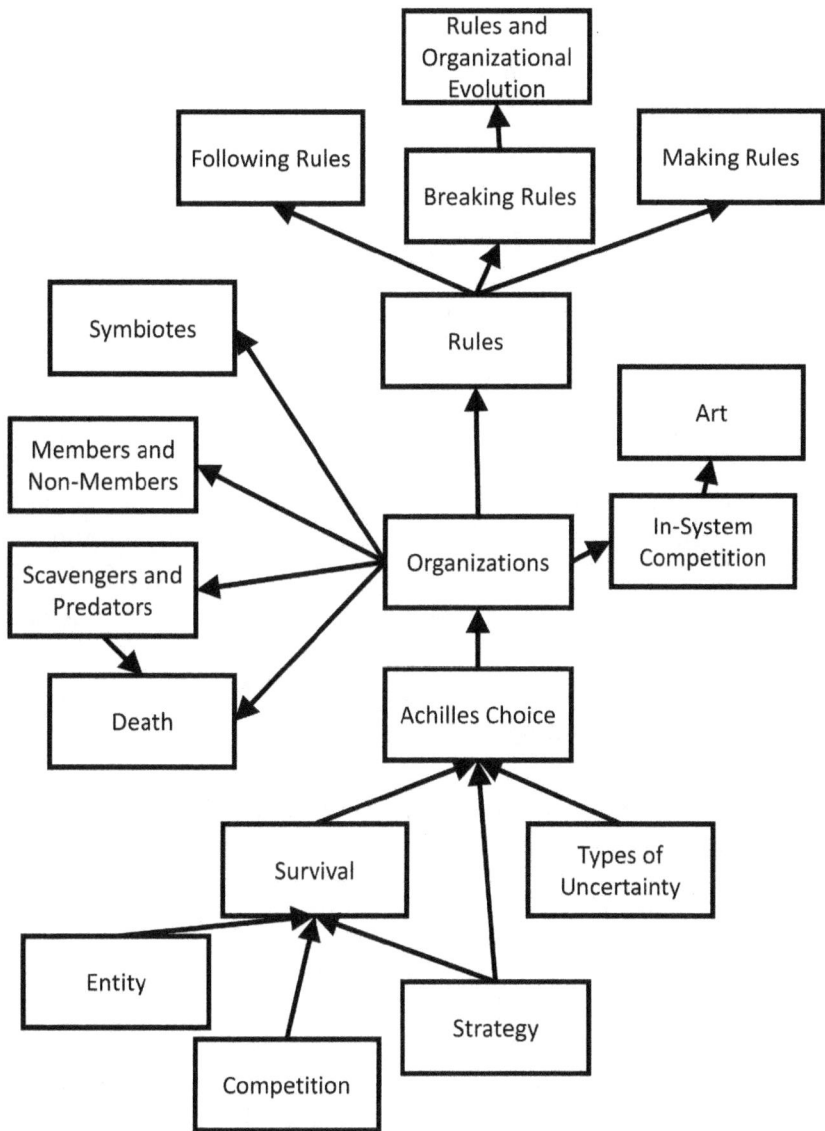

Figure 2.1: Map of Main Concepts

is Achilles Choice - each entity can choose to go alone and have a short and eventful life, or can collaborate with other entities to have a long(er) but less eventful life.

- An organization arises when some entities choose to have longer and less eventful lives. Thus they organize together to share the resources from any win that each of them gets on any day.

- Members and non-members are defined by each organization.

- Symbiotes comprising collaborating non-members are useful for an organization's existence.

- Chapter 5: The need to compete even within an organization leads to the development of in-system competitions within an organization. These explicit or implicit competitions eliminate the possibility of death while still declaring a winner. In-system competitions usually require entities to dedicate significant time and resources to increasing the chances of winning.

- Art is defined as any in-system competition where a win confers no direct functional value, but often a lot of social value from winning itself.

- Chapter 6: Rules (including norms) govern members and membership in organizations. This necessitates the creation of an overhead (or resource tax) dedicated to creating and implementing rules. Following rules may often be a public badge of membership of the organization.

- Rule-breakers arise as soon as there are rules (or norms). An action can break a rule only after the rule is born. Some rule-breakers act out of ignorance, while others consciously break rules.

- Organizational evolution comes from rule-breakers by forcing the organization to either define rules where none existed, or to modify old or less useful rules.

- A balance between following rules and modifying rules is essential to sustaining an organization.

- Organizational dead ends (lone wolves[4]) are entities who do not join organizations. Such entities may sometimes disrupt existing organizations.

- Chapter 7: Scavengers and predators are the natural outcome of early organizational attempts when organizations reuse parts of previous failed organizational attempts.

- Chapter 8: "Natural" organizational death happens when either its entities can no longer cooperate, or when it can no longer get enough resources to cover the overhead of staying organized. "Premature" organizational death happens from predators from the current level, or from predators from other levels.

- Organizational success leads to proliferation of similar organizations in its environment, either from other similar groups of cooperating entities, or from the copies of the first organization that figures out how to replicate.

- Thus, the organization itself becomes the entity in the next layer of complexity. Define this group of organizations as the new layer, and repeat from the top.

Once we understand all the concepts and relations in this map, then we are ready to dive in and apply this framework to what we see around us. We may apply this framework to the general questions posed at the start of this chapter, as well as many other related questions.

In Part II, we will explore some of the implications of this framework. This proceeds as follows:

---

[4]Lone wolves are different from other entities like rule breakers, predators or scavengers.

- Chapter 11 explores some instances of how various aspects covered in Part I can be seen in nature, including in human organizations and groups.

- Chapters 12-15 present some possible rules of behavior for entities in the context of where they are located in relation to organizations.

- Chapters 16-18 end this discussion by exploring what this means for human beings, since we all live in the context of very large organizations, even when we may not belong to a specific one.

Chapter 3

Entities, Competition and Strategy

In this chapter we will describe three basic building blocks that will be the fundamental terms we will use to describe any specific layer.

The first concept is the entity, which is the focus of the framework. Much of what happens in each layer is based on how the entity behaves, and why it does certain things.

The second building block is the process of competition, which seems to exist everywhere from a serene forest to the shark-infested waters of Wall Street (we use such analogies in common speech too).

The final building block is strategy, which is simply the very unique way in which an entity goes about navigating its environment and what it uses as its playbook for competition (playbook is itself a term borrowed from sports competitions). The main concepts covered in this chapter are highlighted in Figure 3.1.

As you read this chapter some of the questions you may ask about your chosen context are listed below. These questions are guidelines to ensure that we have understood the context and the creatures that inhabit it. Sometimes the answer is obvious. Sometimes we have an idea of what the answer can be. In many cases we have to go and find the answers, because we have (personally) never asked the question in this specific context.

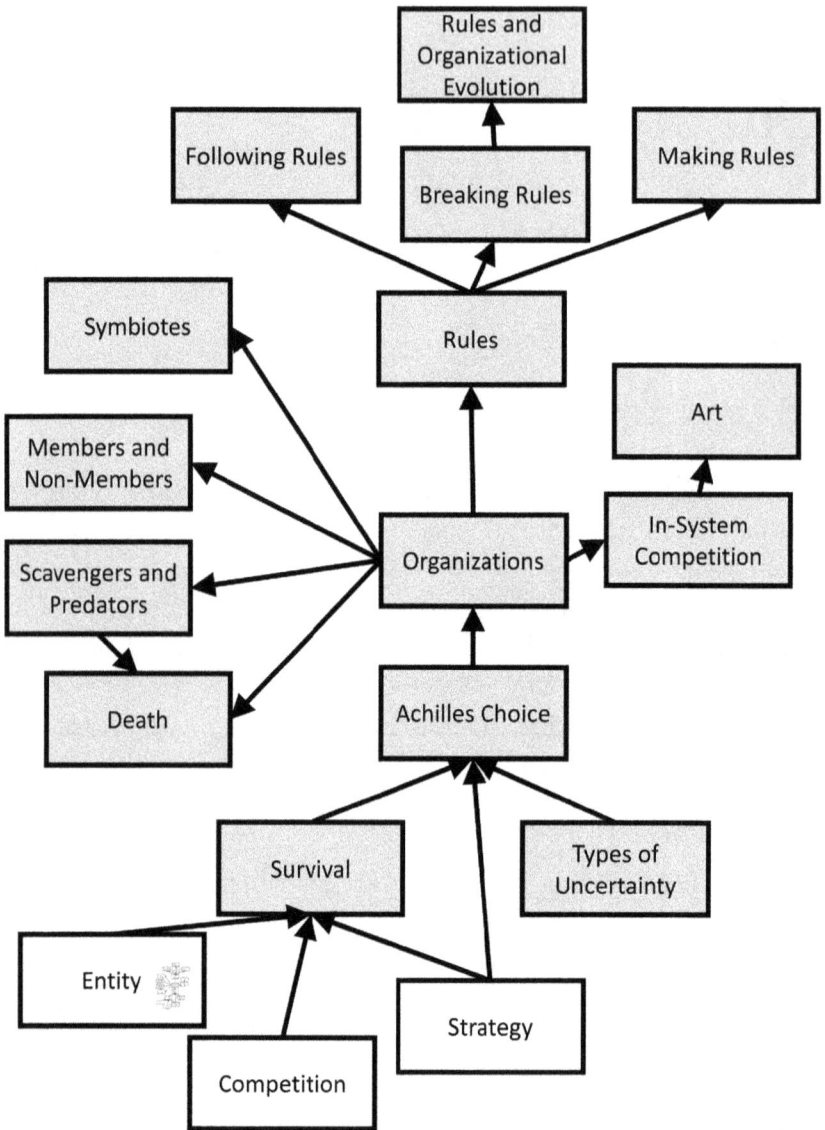

Figure 3.1: Chapter 3 Map: Entities, Competition and Strategy

- What is the context and the specific environment?

- What is the entity in this context? Is there only one entity in this specific area, or are there many?

- How are new entities born, how do they reproduce, and how do they die?

- What are these entities competing for?

- Is there structured competition, or is it unstructured?

- Is this an explicit competition with rules and norms, or does competition have no rules at all? (This looks forward to Chapter 6 which deals with rules.)

- How do we know which entity has "won" a specific competition?

- Is there a behavioral pattern that is clearly identifiable as a specific entity's competitive style? That is, do some entities have unique strategies?

- What is the source of the strategy for a specific entity (that is, where is it written down or encoded)?

- How do entities come up with new strategies?

Some questions appear to be silly because the answer is obvious. If we are talking about deer in a forest, well, of course, we know how they are born, how they reproduce and how they die. We also know that almost all their behavior is derived from their DNA.

Some questions appear to be silly because they appear to be irrelevant. For the deer in the forest, what do we even mean by a specific deer's strategy? It may appear to the layman that all deer are pretty much identical- they live in herds, eat grass and leaves, give birth to fawns, and eventually die or are eaten by predators (or hung as trophies; same result). There is little difference in their strategies, one may say. However, during our hunter-gatherer phase, we humans used to follow herds as they migrated across the land and could identify many different behaviors in the individuals in a herd.

Take another context, and the relevance of the questions changes. For example, take companies. A company is an entity. We know they are born, i.e. created by founders, and they often die, e.g. by going bankrupt.

But how do companies reproduce? What are the rules of their competitions? How many of these rules are written down? Do some companies use the same strategies over and over again when competing against other companies? Where are these strategies written down? How do companies come up with new strategies?

With a change of context the same questions are no longer trivial.

3.1   Entity

Let us start with the concept of the entity.

We assume that entities exist. They don't have to, in which case there is nothing to be discussed. There are many environments in which entities of our interest do not exist. For instance there are no known living organisms on the Earth's moon[1]. It is possible that we can change that in the future.

For each layer we have listed in Chapter 2, there are entities. In the quantum layer the entities have strange names borrowed from regular English words (with no correspondence to the meanings of the original words). In the atomic and molecular layer, there are atoms and molecules. At the cellular level, these entities are cells, and at the multi cellular level, these are plants, animals and insects. In a capitalist economy the entities are the companies that provide us products and services. Whatever the choice of the layer is, there are entities which are an integral part of that layer.

Each layer allows for the possibility of many similar entities

---

[1]While entities of our interest may not exist in an environment, entities of other types always exist. For example, while there are no living organisms on the Earth's Moon, there are certainly molecules, atoms and subatomic particles present there, which are entities in earlier layers.

that can coexist in a specific environment. Each of these entities is born, and will eventually die. Atoms may seem permanent, yet we are familiar with many fearsome processes that rearrange them, consuming and releasing vast amounts of energy. Molecules are constantly being broken apart and reassembled in all living beings and in the terrestrial environments around us. Cells are created and destroyed every minute within our bodies.

Why are entities born? It is probably because birth is an efficient way for existing entities to transfer strategies in the specific environment. Here is an example. At a microscopic level an individual bacterium which has landed in a puddle of food cannot grow beyond a certain size since the chemical processes that govern its internal mechanisms need a certain amount of cellular surface for each unit of volume within the bacteria. Thus, as the bacteria grows larger it makes sense to divide into two and conquer the food.

As ridiculous as it may sound, entities often can be born spontaneously too. When a profitable commercial opportunity arises it can often seem that entrepreneurs arise "out of the woodwork". The seeds of scanning for profitable opportunities are there in every working human, and in a nurturing environment many entrepreneurs try their luck for the first time.

Why do entities die? Let us hold off on this question. We will have more to say about death later on in Chapter 8. As a preview, entities may die from "natural" causes, which assumes that they have a "natural" lifetime (or a range of possible lifetimes), or they may die from "unnatural" causes which makes their lifetime shorter than what can be considered "natural".

From a strategic and organizational perspective death from either natural or unnatural causes is the result of degradation of the level of organization. This results in the dissociation of the entity into the constituent entities of earlier layers. Thus, when a cell dies it may dissociate into complex molecules (e.g. when it dies in the stomach of its predator), or break down into simpler molecules (when it is attacked by a virus), or even into single atoms (if it happens to fall into some bleaching agent, or be near a nuclear reaction).

23

Similarly, when a company "dies", it may dissociate into parts that are incorporated into other companies, or it may break down into individual humans who no longer work together. In the US in the 1980s, it was very popular for enterprising folks to buy up companies, carve them up and sell them to other companies as individual parts. They would also "discard" the pieces that they could not sell. This process continues today too, but does not attract much attention since the number of potentially bloated targets is much smaller (precisely because the corporate raiders are always looking for opportunities).

It is also interesting to conjecture about the similarities and differences between the birth, lifespan and death of entities across different layers. Some cells have shorter natural lives than multicellular creatures, and perhaps we can argue that some molecules have shorter lives than the cells that they belong to. On the other hand, there are many molecules that retain their form much longer than cells- perhaps a water molecule in an ocean. It depends upon the environment and the context. In the human world individuals often live longer than many of the startup firms and community organizations they participate in. On the other hand, there are also many stable organizations which span multiple human lives- for example, countries, large companies, and some religious institutions.

Which was the first entity to be born in a specific layer? Well, we will have more to say about that later on in Section 6.5. To look ahead, the process which starts at one layer and then logically arrives at the next layer of organization describes the birth of the "first" entity of the next layer. While there will technically always be a "first," it is certainly plausible that environmental conditions allow for multiple similar entities to independently form in a short period of time. To see the birth of the "first" entity in a specific layer we have to zoom in and consider the entities in the "previous" layer. Thus, to consider the "first" molecule, we must look at how atoms behave. To see the birth of the first cell we must learn about how molecules behave. To see the creation of the first company we must see how humans behave.

Thus, there are entities.

3.2 Competition

As soon as one entity comes into existence in an environment, it is very likely that there are multiple similar entities within the confines of that environment (as long as the environment is stable and does not change). This may happen due to multiple spontaneous entity births, or through some form of imitation or replication. No matter how large the environment is, the geometric growth of replicating entities can fill it up pretty soon. When all options to spread out have been exhausted, these entities must now compete[2] against each other.

What is a desirable resource that entities will compete for? For a large range of entities- cells, multi cellular organisms and plants, insects and animals- the answer is simple. They compete for food, energy and living space. If they reproduce sexually, then they also compete for desirable partners.

How do molecules, atoms and earlier layers compete? Perhaps subatomic particles compete for quarks, or for some form of energy. Perhaps organic molecules compete for more carbon atoms.

From the cellular level onward there is conventional competition as we understand it. Cells, animals and social organizations compete for food at the most basic level. Plants compete for sunlight and water. Tigers compete for herds of deer.

Social groups compete for human members, and religions compete for followers. Online social networks compete for members and the time they spend online, as well as for companies which will come to their platform and pay advertising dollars.

Countries used to fight for colonies just a couple of centuries ago. Nowadays multinational firms compete for business across global markets.

There is competition everywhere on earth. Your backyard is the scene of devastating battles played out between different plants, albeit over months and years. Gardeners soon discover

---

[2]We will consider symmetric competition here, which is competition between entities in the same layer, e.g. bacteria vs other cells. In Chapter 7 we will consider asymmetric competition, which is competition between entities from different layers, e.g. viruses and cells, or bacteria and animals.

that every plant has the capacity to be invasive and overrun other plants around it.

Why do entities compete? The simplest answer is to survive and grow. To grow as a physical entity, and then to propagate, and then let their progeny grow.

Why do entities need to grow? After all, they don't have to. In various corners everywhere we can find instances of entities that arise but do not wish to grow. Not every neutron is part of an atom, not every atom belongs to a molecule, and not every cell belongs to a multi cellular creature.

However only those entities that wish to live and grow will get a chance to do so. You do not have to have any consciousness in order to grow or compete. Organic molecules, single cells and many other entities have grown and competed without any consciousness or intelligence (in the conventional human sense).

In the long run, only those who happened to grow have increased their numbers, and allowed for the possibility of the next level of organization. There is no judgment if such an entity does not wish to grow. The universe does not really care, but the universe is also full of only those entities which wish to grow and prosper.

Thus, entities compete.

3.3 Strategy

3.3.1 What is a Strategy?

Competition makes life difficult for all the entities in an environment. Without competition an entity could easily find plentiful food and other resources all around it. With competition it must now take action once in a while to ensure that it gets enough resources.

Every entity engages in deliberate actions to try to ensure its own long term survival. When its own actions are coordinated over time in some manner (whether consciously or accidentally), we will define this as the entity's strategy.

An entity's actions to find resources and tackle competition have a structure, a pattern, or perhaps a method. Do these actions really have to have a pattern or a structure? Probably not - it is just that any patterns which do not support a functional or competitive goal would lose out to the more "successful" patterns over generations. This happens due to the cumulative effect of even tiny advantages over "long" periods of time.

For instance, if a particular strategy provides an entity a mere 0.1% advantage in resource gathering, then over a few hundred generations that entity's offspring will almost entirely prevail in numbers over others. To provide some perspective a bacterial generation is about an hour, and an insect generation is about a season. Bacteria have been competing for about a billion years or two, and insects for a few hundred million years. Over such long periods of time, tiny advantages can really add up.

The universe does not care if an entity has a strategy or not. There is no value judgment from the universe if an entity wishes to depend upon random chance to gather the resources needed to live and procreate. However, not surprisingly, only the progeny of those who actively wish to survive have a chance at survival in the long run. Consider a plant or a coral which is rooted to one spot all its life. It too tries to use different ways of scattering its seeds so that they spread to different areas. Most seeds die, but enough survive.

If some entities want to "get away from it all" and live the simple life, that too is a strategy. It helps the species go and gain footholds in other environments. Perhaps it will help survival when rainfall patterns change, or when the next meteor strikes earth.

3.3.2   The Measure of Success

Strategic success, of course, is measured in only one way: survival over the long term. The really long term.

Each possible set of strategies is associated with a time scale, from milliseconds to decades. This depends on the specific survival problem the entity is faced with. The response of a deer when immediately targeted by a tiger occurs on a different timescale than that of a bear facing winter. The strategy timescale is also related to the typical lifetime of the entity. For example, a proton may live for billions of years, or may have a lifetime of milliseconds. A molecule in the ocean may retain its identity for millions of years, but one in the human body may last for just a few hours.

Irrespective of the lifetime of an entity, the strategic success of that entity's actions is measured at every possible timescale. The entity, or it's kin, must survive for ever.

Success is defined quite starkly: survive. Survive today, survive a hundred years from now and survive for eternity, even if members of your species are individually short-lived. On a related note, we are all short-lived.

3.3.3   Where is Strategy Written?

If every entity has a strategy, and if some entities can have different strategies than others, then we should explore where the strategy is stored within the entity.

Even when it is not explicitly written down, the strategy an entity follows may arise from natural forces playing out over its form and structure. Thus, strategy may follow from fundamental physical forces. When a long inorganic polymer is forming, various forces of attraction and dispersion ensure that simpler monomers in the environment find their way to the growth end and are incorporated in the polymer. If there are two polymers to "choose" from, the monomer goes towards that which is more attractive due to distance and molecular orientation. For organic polymers these simpler chemical forces are mediated by very specific cellular environments which nudge the molecules to behave in a certain manner.

At some point in time there must have existed a transition stage between chemical entities and cellular entities. These may perhaps be described as cells without any genetic code, a cell trying to manage itself using only the tools of the earlier (molecular) level. There is probably very little this entity could do to repeat certain actions that were successful, since there was no way of remembering them. When did the full transition happen, to involve genetic material? Probably when small snippets of nucleic acid, which have no direct function, were nevertheless found to influence the creation of some bio-molecules, and hence represented a form of memory and repeatability. Imagine how subtle this effect may have been, and yet how this formed the basis for DNA as we know it today.

At the cellular level we can already see complex interdependent interactions between the molecules within the cell which coordinate the response to "external" molecular signals. The difference between a molecular strategy and a cellular strategy lies in the complexity and variety of possible actions and patterns of actions.

There are two broad types of cells: those with genetic material spread all over inside the cell, and those with genetic material enclosed in a nucleus within the cell. Since both of these exist, we can only assume that there is still some benefit to not having a nucleus. However, there are no multi-cellular organisms that are composed of cells without nucleus. Or perhaps there are, and we have not found them.

We can list many examples of strategy stored in genetic material. There are colonies of single-celled slime that are have no cellular differentiation that are still able to target resources and "solve" mazes to find food. All multi-cellular animals know instinctively how to breathe, digest food, and similarly execute many of the physiological functions that coordinate millions of cells in the different parts and systems of their body. Many birds instinctively know how to build nests, and insects know how to move in a pattern on the jungle floor that allows them to find food over a specific area.

But strategy can also come from cognition and intelligence. Amphibians and reptiles react to their environment in broadly predefined ways based on their brain wiring. Dolphins, primates, elephants and many other creatures have the brainpower to be able to think and learn from their environment and react to it with thought. Thus the difference between a DNA-based strategy and a brain-based strategy is, again, in the complexity, variety and flexibility of possible actions and patterns of actions.

When we get to higher levels, e.g. social entities or business entities, it is interesting to find out where the coding of the organization may exist. Human social groups may react to opportunities based on their capabilities and working relations which transcend the arrival or departure of individual members in the group. A fast food business may ensure standardization and scalability by specifying each and every operation in a 500-page operating manual, with regular audits to ensure compliance. A bureaucracy may have explicit and implicit rules and norms about behavior and responses to specific actions and events.

Some startups may reinvent the mundane business processes of creating order forms, check and balances and approval procedures that any business needs in order to operate. Some organizations depend upon off-the-shelf software packages to do these standard tasks. Large organizations may choose to devise their own processes and hire system architects to construct these process systems. Each of these has strategic implications for many businesses.

A tiger does not consciously think of breathing or digestion when it is chasing down a prey. Similarly, a large corporation depends upon the standard business processes to be working efficiently when it is closing deals with other large firms or governments.

Thus, strategy is "written" in the physics of our atoms, in the chemistry of our molecules, in the DNA of our cells, in the wiring of our brains, and in our structured interactions with our hive sisters.

3.3.4 Strategy and Population Evolution

The responses of the entire population of entities to changes in the environment is an interesting phenomenon as well.

Environments inevitably change, sometimes suddenly and sometimes gradually. One element of an entity's strategy is also the search for variations of a successful strategy she can use to exploit the slightly different conditions at the edges of each environment. The conditions inside these niches are not as favorable. Perhaps there is less food, perhaps the sun shines only six months in a year. The same basic strategy can be modified to allow for these variations. For example, the basic opportunity provided by sunlight is captured using chlorophyll, soil and air by all plants on earth. However their other characteristics vary widely. Some cacti take years to grow a few inches, while bamboo can grow more than a foot a day.

By their very presence entities change the environment. Sometimes they change the environment quite radically. Consider the time in prehistory when some cells discovered how to use the energy of the sun to break carbon dioxide. The toxic byproduct was oxygen, which is a rather corrosive gas. While initially it was not a problem, in a relatively "short" time the atmosphere was full of so much oxygen that whole kingdoms of cells perished. Some descendants of such cells exist around the deep sea volcanic vents where they still utilize the sulfuric energy sources that the earlier generations of cells were based on, a couple of billion years ago.

When the environment changes it is often the various niches which provide some hope for survival. Even if such cataclysmic events occur once every hundred million years they will still wipe out all populations with strategies that ignore the unfavorable niches.

There are times when the population focuses on certain types of strategies as the primary means of expansion. These are the four types of environments:

- In a stable sparsely populated environment (i.e., where resources are much greater than what the current population can use), the population can undergo periods of rapid expansion. This is when the current strategies are replicated as fast as possible, with the fast replicators getting a larger share of the environment.

- In a stable crowded environment the population is forced to complete with each other, and this may lead to large changes in strategies. Thus, the crowding of the environment itself makes it a different environment even though it has the same external characteristics. For example, a crowded forest may be no different from an "empty" meadow in terms of the basic soil composition, rainfall and sunshine it receives. However, it will be a completely different environment for a tree simply because there are so many trees.

- In an unstable sparse environment it is possible that a species that focuses on quickly sharing viable variations has a better chance of surviving. In this manner only those populations that share strategy or genetic variations have some hope of finding a strategy that finally works well.

- Finally, in an unstable crowded environment quick sharing of genetic variations is important and we can also expect a radical decimation of many entities and elimination of outdated strategies.

3.3.5   Replication and Strategy Modification

Replication allows for the exponential growth of stable organizations, as well as the development of strategic variations when the process of replication is imperfect.

Strategy modification is an important aspect of competition. Without varying strategies, all entities would be subject to the same environmental risks. Replication is a complex process, even when it looks simple.

Entities that have stumbled upon structured sharing (i.e. sexual reproduction) of viable mutations (i.e. variations in encoded strategy) can also compete for partners. From the cellular layer onward sexual reproduction is an important advantage. Life replicated asexually for a few billions of years and stayed at the level of unicellular bacteria and algae-like creatures. Something happened at a point in Earth's prehistory which caused multi-cellular life forms to move from the oceans on to the land. One conjecture is that the precipitating event may have been sexual reproduction- a structured way of sharing viable strategy variations across similar entities. This process greatly accelerated the exploration of viable alternative designs of entities for the many environmental conditions all over the earth. This made life more robust to environmental variations.

Do atoms replicate? Perhaps- if you consider all possible changes in atoms from fusion and fission. Over long periods of time the neutrons and protons may circle back and form another atom of similar structure. In certain cases the environmental conditions can be more conducive to the formation of a particular kind of atom. Deep within the sun nuclear reactions convert hydrogen into helium. This is not replication in the sense that a bacterium is splitting into two bacteria. However, the end result is quite similar. At the end of the process we now have more helium atoms than we did earlier.

All entities that cannot replicate will live out their lifespan and dissociate back into entities of an earlier layer. Thus, many entities will take birth spontaneously and live and die without replicating as long as the environment stays favorable.

An entity may eventually "figure out" how to replicate. Perhaps this, too, is also a long story of trial and error. Perhaps "replication" can happen only after the death of the entity, when the earlier components are more likely to reform into another entity because of their memory or history of having participated in the recently demised entity. When a cell dies, its components are often reused by other cells, including, perhaps its DNA. When a firm collapses, the employees of the firm may choose to get together and form their own startup. This startup may utilize similar internal operations and processes and external relationships from the earlier firm.

Thus, "soon" there are multiple entities within the confines of a particular environment. These entities may have kinship or other similarities. They are very rarely all identical. In an extreme case even if they are exactly identical, they exist at different physical points in the environment. Some may have access to richer sources of sustenance, and some may be close to the fringe of the livable conditions in this niche.

Thus, entities compete using strategies.

Chapter 4

The Organization

In this chapter we will explain the emergence of organizations. Organizations are collections of individual entities, and are usually much smaller than the entire population. Organizations can be as ad-hoc or as structured as needed. Thus, a group of atoms who "organize" into a molecule, and a few college mates who join together to create a startup are both examples of organizations.

So, why do entities organize?

We have already introduced the reality that entities compete, and that differences in their strategies can account for their cumulative successes or failures. It is quite tempting at this point to consider a Darwinian world where the survival of the fittest is the only principle that counts.

Yet, the world is not so.

Most of the entities around us survive based on the characteristics of the organizations they belong to, rather than their own attributes in relation to the environment they inhabit[1]. Extremely unstable molecules that would have no chance of "surviving" in the wild can still exist for long periods of time inside living cells. A successful dance company usually employs a large number of good dancers while a superlative dancer starves "outside" searching for individual fame.

---

[1]If we define the organization itself as the environment, then the entity is naturally suited to the environment- an example of entities creating their own micro environment.

As we read this chapter, some of the questions we should apply to our discussion to are:

- What challenges does competition create for an entity?

- What strategy must an entity follow to "win" in the short term[2], e.g. a few hours? In the medium term, e.g. a few weeks? In the long term, e.g. a year? In the really long term, e.g. a decade?

- What constitutes a win in the longest term we are willing to consider?

- What does day-to-day success mean when an entity is working alone, versus when an entity is working as a member of a group, for example when foraging for food in a forest?

- What are the pros and cons of competing alone, compared to competing as a member of a group?

- How do we know that an entity belongs to an organization?

While we focus on the organization itself in this chapter, subsequent chapters will cover further discussions on the members, as well as the rules and the health of the organization (as opposed to the health of the entity). The main concepts covered in this chapter are highlighted in Figure 4.1.

4.1   The Nature of Competition

Competition is difficult. At every level and at all times it poses various challenges for the entity. We will break down our broad study of competition into a few pieces.

First we discuss timescales and determine that survival is the relevant success measure in the longest timescale an entity can influence using its strategy.

---

[2]Short term needs to be defined in context of the entity's lifespan- for a bacterium short term may be a few seconds.

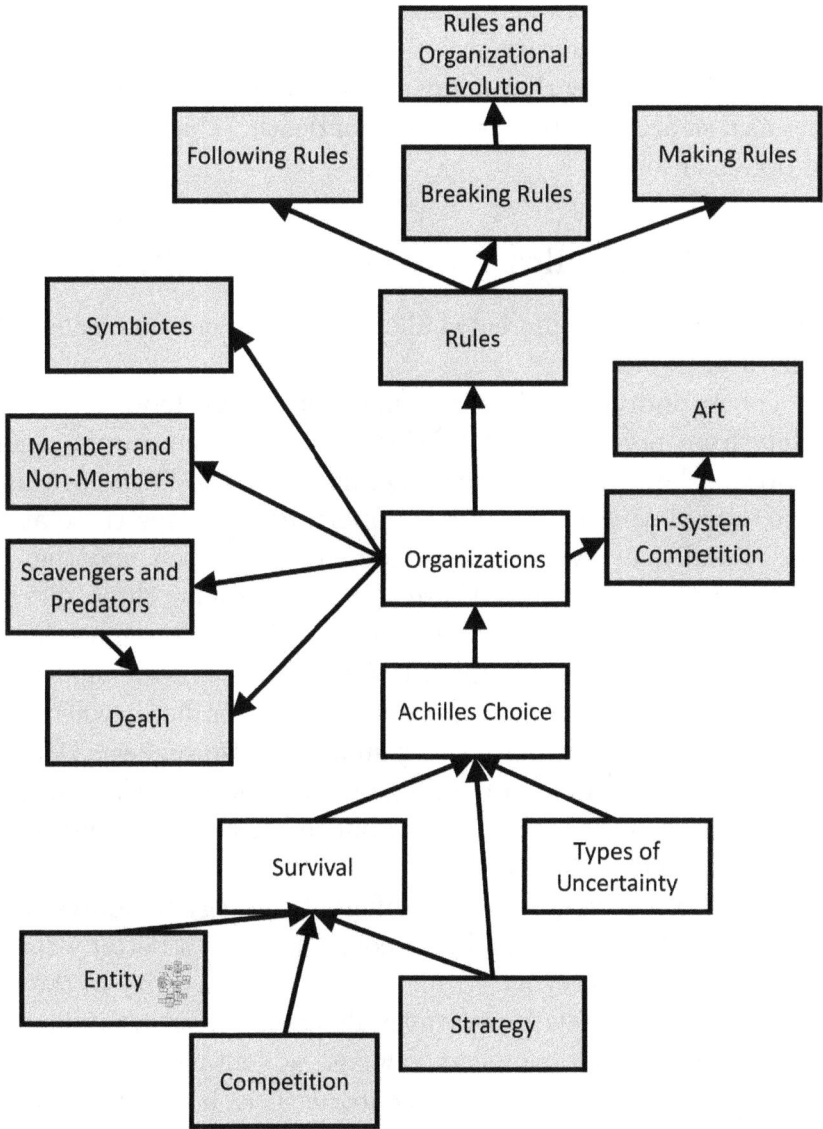

Figure 4.1: Chapter 4 Map: Types of Uncertainty, Survival and Organizations

Next we consider the main factor that stands in the way of survival- uncertainty. We consider its nature and the main sources of uncertainty for an entity, and show that the largest source of uncertainty for an entity are other entities most similar to itself.

Finally, we show that many entities cooperate with other entities as a strategy to reduce the risk of death. This forms the basis of organizations.

4.1.1   Timescales

Competition poses different challenges at different timescales. Consider a pack of deer.

For an individual deer, the main needs are food, mates and safety from predators. Thus, if she does not find any food for a few days, she will die. On the other hand, the herd faces predators once every few weeks, and it is important to escape these attack too. Finally, every year there is a mating season and the deer needs to find a mate[3]. These are problems on three different timescales- daily, weekly and annually. Each deer must have a strategy to survive the competitive challenge at each timescale.

Does the deer stay on the outskirts of the herd, where food is better, but the risk of getting hunted is also higher? Does the male deer focus more on building larger antlers which provide an advantage during mating season, but are heavier and need to be carried around all year long?

Each deer utilizes a slightly different strategy to address these questions[4]. If an individual deer comes up with a better strategy, it has a better chance at leaving behind more progeny in the next generation. In a few generations almost all deer will follow the strategy which today appears new and advantageous.

Life is not simple for the predator either. It too needs to find food (the deer, in this case), mates, and survive disease and illness

---

[3]As a reminder, every deer need not seek out mates. However, only those that seek out mates will have a chance of leaving progeny after they die. In a few generations we will no longer have deer who do not want to procreate.

[4]Survival is determined not just by strategy but also by execution of that strategy. Strategy does not exist without execution.

caused by other organisms. On the other side of the food chain, life is not simple for the grass and trees either. They too need to grow in locations with fertile soil, water and sunshine; they too need to discourage predators like deer, and they too must figure out how to procreate.

In the world of business the timescale of the decision also plays a very important role. A firm may choose to pursue market share in the short term, and revert to pursuing profits in the medium term.

Consider a retailer selling baked products. Every hour customers walk in, and the employees have to decide how to serve them- when to bake fresh batches, which products to run promotions on, and how to schedule cleaning and other activities in the shop. Every day and every week the supervising manager has to consider predicted customer traffic and schedule the work hours of all the employees over the next few weeks. On a monthly basis she also has to consider hiring more employees with specific skills. Every few months she may have to decide whether to add equipment, rent more space, figure out suppliers for the ingredients. Finally, every year she may have to decide if the current location and number of storefronts is suitable for the profitability and growth of the business. On an even longer timescale, say a few years, she may have to consider if people are changing their dietary preferences, as well as how the local economy (or, for that matter, the global economy) is doing.

As the duration over which specific decisions play out becomes longer, the ability to predict success or failure for specific strategies becomes more difficult. Uncertainties become more severe. Simpler objectives like the availability of food, safety, security and other goals become more difficult to predict. The consequence of a specific action now becomes much more difficult to link to outcomes that won't occur until a long time in the future. The environment may change. The herd may be larger, or smaller. There may be different predators, and different diseases.

4.1.2 Survival

Every strategy that appears attractive in the near future also must still work out for longer timescales.

First of all, the entity must overcome hunger or some immediate need. Thus, a zebra must look for food every day. Similarly, a retailer must look for customers every day, or at least every week. It must compete with other entities which want the same resources- the zebra competes with other zebras, deer, cows, giraffes, and even elephants. A retailer must compete with other retailers selling similar products, different products, and even those selling services.

However, a strategy that meets this immediate need by increasing the risks in the long term is clearly not a good strategy. For example, the retailer can increase immediate profitability by reducing the quality of its products, but this carries with it the risk of permanently losing customers when they find out that the products do not last as long as expected.

The only sensible long-term competitive goal is survival[5].

If we deconstruct the strategy playbook of any entity, we will find survival tactics for every timescale within it. Some of these strategies will also be longer than the lifetime of the entity. In this playbook we will also find traces of its ancestral strategic choices based on the history of threats they faced in the past.

An additional problem is the need to modify the strategy in the face of changing environments. The entity must ensure that even if its strategy is hard-wired, it still has some way of modifying its strategy since the world around it will eventually change.

If the entity's entire strategy is completely hard-coded at birth, then the only way to modify the strategy is through mutation and replication.

Strategies vary depending on the layer the entity belongs to. At the cellular level individual cells have their strategy hard-coded into their genetic material, with the provision that specific en-

---

[5]Once again, this is not necessarily conscious for the entity- only those strategies which improve long-term survival of an entity will remain in a population.

vironmental conditions may switch on certain segments of their genetic material. This is a relatively simple way of changing an entire sequence of responses to the same immediate criteria in a different context. This is the result of the entity retaining past experiences in its strategic memory.

Multi-cellular organisms with nervous systems (like small fishes and reptiles) respond to environmental signals. This includes vibration, contact, sound and light and other sensory input to their brain. This perception of specific elements in their immediate environment determines their responses. Their specific responses are often inherited, rather than learned. Thus these too are an extension of the genetic code that shows a qualitative increase in complexity from the molecular level.

Finally, through memory and cognition, primates can learn the attractiveness or risks of specific things in their environment and pass that on to the social group. This socially-transferred strategy exists in addition to any hard-coded responses.

In every layer, all of this strategy is geared towards long-term survival.

4.2   Uncertainty

What prevents an entity from surviving? Why does it even need a strategy?

Uncertainty.

Yesterday there was a nice fruit tree here, but today it has no fruits. Yesterday this watering hole was safe, but today there may be hyenas hiding nearby. Last year this place had a lot of sun and rain, but today it is too dry. Last Christmas customers wanted to buy our products, but this year they do not like the styles we want to sell.

Uncertainty requires a strategy. Only the first (and only) entity in an environment can get by with no strategy. The resources seem so bountiful that all it needs to do is sit in one place and eat till full. However, who knows where the bounty comes from. Perhaps tomorrow the source will dry up, or the winds may change direction. In the absence of a strategy the entity will die at the first sign of uncertainty.

Sometimes the strategy itself will precipitate uncertainty. After the discovery or revelation of a successful strategy the environment changes rapidly (if the entities can replicate). In fact, the reason the environment changes so rapidly is that a successful strategy has been found. Thus, the initial euphoria for the followers of the successful strategy is a transient state. Very soon, the world goes back to being competitive, with parity among similar entities. Thus, an important consideration in an entity's strategy has to be the degree of change in its environment. Even if the particular entity has not faced a particular change in its environment, over generations many of the context changes faced by its ancestors get encoded in its hard-wired strategies. An event that happens once every ten generations will get encoded- perhaps in the entity's DNA, perhaps in social memory or perhaps as old wives tales, myths or parables.

We will attempt to broadly classify all the uncertainty an entity faces. This classification of types of uncertainty is necessarily subjective. For our purpose three types will suffice.

4.2.1 Uncertainty of the First Type

Uncertainty of the first type involves random events that are influenced by nothing in their environment. If there is anything we can do to influence the occurrence of the random event, it is no longer an uncertain event of the first type.

There are actually very few instances of the first type of uncertainty, which can be considered completely independent random events. One possible example of this is the decay event of a single radioactive atom on earth far away from other radioactive matter. This is a random event influenced by very little in its environment. Even on earth, if we put a sufficient number of these together, we can detonate an atom bomb. This means that all of them decay almost at the same time, so they are not independent. Similarly, at the center of the sun such an atom would be bombarded with so much matter and energy that it would have no chance to stay stable.

Thus, this first type of uncertainty is very much a conceptual type, and has very little relevance to our discussion.

4.2.2 Uncertainty of the Second Type

Uncertainty of the second type covers random events that are caused by the interaction of various physical objects in the environment. Here we explicitly account for the interaction between objects due to "simple" fundamental physical interactions, like gravity, electromagnetism, radiation and other forces. Thus, many of the well-studied examples are to be found in the area of physics and related sciences.

This type of uncertainty is really difficult to predict since there are many interacting elements and processes involving energy and different states of matter. Even the simplest models of physical systems result in chaotic outcomes[6]. The study of chaos has transformed our understanding of the natural world, and has also been greatly facilitated by increasingly capable computers.

It is much easier to find examples of the second kind of uncertainty, which is caused by the literally mind-less interaction of matter and energy. An example of this is the weather pattern on a planet with no life. For example, the Giant Red Spot on the planet Jupiter is a four-century long storm. It is the result of uncertainty of the second type. While a weather system is quite difficult to model, even simpler systems exhibit this type of uncertainty. For example, we have not been able to model the motion of three bodies in space- we can only simulate it using computers. Even then our confidence in such a simulation does not extent very far out into the future.

Our attempts to predict the future, even in sandbox conditions

---

[6]Chaos has been equated in the popular narrative as the butterfly effect. This has been wrongly described as the ability of butterfly to cause a hurricane. To put it in the proper context, the butterfly wing can merely change the occurrence of hurricanes in the season (e.g. in August instead of September). It cannot create new hurricanes if there would have been none in the first place.

(i.e. by building simple physical models using mathematics and a lot of computers) become less accurate the further into the future we try to predict. Our best efforts so far have been able to predict the weather on earth only up to about three to five days. It still needs a lot of tweaking in order to try to fit the predictions to previous examples of known weather. Our attempts to predict the paths of asteroids (in order to figure out if any will hit the earth) suffer from a similar accuracy problem on a longer timescale (centuries instead of days).

Uncertainty of the second type affects all entities. All living cells, plants and animals are subject to the chaotic movement of water and air over the surface of the planet. To explain this chaos, early civilizations believed that natural forces had a mind of their own, and cared little for the affairs of mortal humans.

Events driven by uncertainties of the second type have influenced the development and evolution of life on earth. They continue to influence our lives through weather patterns on earth as well as sunspots and solar flares from our local star.

4.2.3   Uncertainty of the Third Type

Uncertainty of the third type covers random events which are driven by the strategy of entities. Since the strategy of a cell is ultimately driven by the interaction of its atoms driven by electromagnetic and other forces, uncertainty of the third type is arguably a special kind of uncertainty of the second type.

It is, however qualitatively different. It allows certain elements to have an over-sized influence. For example, a carbon atom in the DNA of a cell can have a disproportionate influence on the behavior of the entire cell compared to a carbon atom which makes up a molecule of carbon dioxide in the atmosphere. We can currently predict the weather for a few days. We are nowhere near being able to model the behavior of a cell at the atomic level. In both cases we have to model the behavior of some components much larger than the atom[7].

---

[7]In the case of the weather, it is large volumes of the atmosphere a few

We can find examples of the third type of uncertainty all around us. An example of the third type of uncertainty is the sales and revenues of any business when there are other similar businesses competing for the same customers. Come to think of it, if there are complex organic molecules in Jupiter's Great Red Spot, then by these definitions, the Great Red Spot too might well be an example of the third type of uncertainty, rather than the second type.

4.2.4 The Fallacy of Conventional Statistics

Much of the machinery used to explain physics and chemistry depends upon the first type of uncertainty. As a consequence, a lot of the statistical tools also assume that any uncertainty is of the first or at best, the second type. In the human world it can be quite a challenge to find any examples of uncertainty of the first type.

Is it possible to determine which type of uncertainty has generated some observed data? For example, consider a cow studying the patterns in the flow of food during its lifetime spent on a farm. If modeled conventionally, this is a very stable system up to the point when the cow is slaughtered for meat. Any uncertainty in the flow of food in a farm comes from uncertainty of the third type, not the first type.

Take the example of business sales prediction. Most existing forecasting software assume that the underlying uncertainty comes from mindless random sources residing in the whims of customers, rather than from other competing firms. However, both the behavior of customers and the behavior of competitors are driven by uncertainties of the third type.

Due to the nature of competitive markets and institutions, assuming uncertainty of the first type works a lot of the time. However, it also tends to fail most spectacularly. The attempt to model commodity market prices in the early 70s led Benoit Mandelbrot to discover that conventional statistics does not work,

---

miles across, and in the case of cells it is the behavior of major organelles in a very simplified manner.

45

and to lay the foundation for the study of chaos theory. Yet we still continue to use conventional statistical analysis to try to analyze events around us, particularly in business.

Conventional statistics forms the basic machinery of a lot of the analysis of competitor sales, prediction of the movement of stock markets, assessing the risk of flooding and fires for housing insurance.

Yet these are examples of uncertainties of the second and third kinds, making conventional statistics the incorrect analysis tool. What makes the process of studying these uncertainties very deceptive is that under many "normal" conditions they all look quite similar to each other. Thus we may be lulled from a few decades of weather data into thinking that there are things called "hundred-year storms", which can be expected to happen only once every hundred years. However, competing humans (and nations) are very much a part of the system, and we have modified the very system that we assume is independent of us when analyzing events.

Try to use statistical analysis to answer this question- "Which piece should a player use in the 15th move to maximize the chance of winning a game of chess?" Current forecasting approaches to answering this question may look at a few thousand games where the opponent's skill level matches the skill level of the opponent we are playing against. Using this data we would then correlate the chances of winning for each of the different observed 15th moves. We are reasonably certain that this approach will not win any competitive game[8].

4.3   The Rise of Cooperation

Much of the philosophy behind this entire framework draws on this idea that in our world almost all the uncertainty we face is of the third type. In this section we will explore what the nature of uncertainty means for the lives of an entity, and how that gives

---

[8]If by some luck this strategy wins some games, it can be uncovered by an opponent, and be used to defeat the player in many more subsequent games.

rise to cooperative behavior[9]. So, let us start with the greatest uncertainty that an entity faces.

4.3.1   The Greatest Uncertainty

An entity faces uncertainty every moment of its life. The uncertainties and consequent decisions that the entity takes may then play out over different timescales, from the immediate to the long term, and can last even beyond the death of the entity itself. Each action is often a balance between the immediate consequences and benefits, and the consequences and benefits at every timescale that is longer than immediate.

This is limited mainly by the predictive capacity of the entity itself. Thus cells may encode some strategies in their own DNA based on their chemical-signal-based understanding of the environment. Many small animals delegate the immediate decisions to a rudimentary brain that integrates visual, auditory and other sensory understanding of their environment, while continuing to depend on their DNA for many long-term decisions.

Consider the relative frequency of the three types of uncertainty that an entity faces.

The first type of uncertainty is so infrequent that it rarely infringes on the agenda for an entity.

Much of the uncertainty faced by an entity is of the second type. For humans, as an example, everyday variations in weather are of this type- rain and clouds are caused by the interaction of innumerable molecules of matter and energy. Far less frequently we can also experience meteor strikes, which are caused by the gravitational interactions between the sun, all the planets, and many rocks moving in between them.

Finally, there is uncertainty of the third type, which is introduced by other entities. For example, early plants completely changed the nature of the atmosphere from soothing nitrogen and

---

[9]This should not be taken to mean that every entity cooperates. There will be some entities who want to fully cooperate with other cooperating entities. At the other extreme, there will be some who want full independence by living the unconnected life. This variation is present in every layer.

sulfur (to the contemporary living creatures) to corrosive oxygen. This lead to the death of almost all species of flora and fauna which depended upon the original atmosphere. Drastic climate change, local or global, is also a relatively rare occurrence. Minor climate change has occurred more frequently in the history of the earth. But all of these are large-scale infrequent events.

Uncertainty of the third type is a little more pervasive than climate change. Any entity spends its day (or minute) on rather mundane pursuits like food, shelter and reproduction. Since most entities live with other similar entities, this boils down to intense competition for these items with other similar entities. Even if they do not want to live in close proximity with other similar entities (like, say, apex predators), sooner or later each entity finds itself restricted to a territory from which it draws food and sustenance, bounded on all sides by either barren territory that serves no purpose, or the territories of other entities. Thus, its life is spent on maintaining the boundaries of this territory against the encroachment from its neighbors.

For herd entities, like bacteria, trees, some species of fish, or herbivores, the competition for food is much more immediate. As they say, the early bird catches the worm (which is instructive for both the bird and the worm). For deer or zebra, the need to get to fresh leaves ahead of the herd has to be tempered with the increased risk of becoming easier prey for predators. Yet the amount of time an individual deer has to spend countering the actions of a predator is dwarfed by the amount of time it spends attempting to find food and mates while living in its herd.

We spend most of our day competing against others who are the most similar to us. Nations compete with each other for influence over even more nations. A fast food company spends most of its time figuring out the actions of other fast food companies. Humans scheme against (or collaborate with) other humans. Molecules of oxygen compete with each other to react with burning cellulose in a fire.

Our greatest uncertainty comes from those who are the most similar to us.

4.3.2 Success is Fickle

Success is difficult in a competitive environment, and she does not visit the same entity every day. Winning on a given day provides no guarantee of winning the next day. Solitary apex predators go many days without eating, interrupted by days where there is too much to eat. Small businesses also live in a very uncertain environment where long periods of struggle may be punctuated with a sudden large contract or viral success on social media[10].

In many cases the competition itself may cause the entity's immediate death from the actions of the competitor. In less severe cases the lack of reward may cause the entity's death due to a lack of food or other resources. Either way, life is tough and death is a constant possibility.

A slightly different strategy is used by wolves or hyenas. A small group of wolves can cooperate in searching out a larger animal that is often too large for a single wolf to capture. Such prey can be successfully captured by the group, and then shared with all members (unequally, based on social hierarchy and hunger). This is interspersed with the smaller but more frequent small prey like rabbits, which may be shared with a smaller part of the group.

Finally, a different strategy is that followed by large groups where each individual follows relatively simple rules to coordinate with the rest of the group to find food or escape predators. Such examples include large flocks of many animals- birds, fish, zebras, as well as some instances of single-celled entities like bacteria and slime molds[11].

4.3.3 Achilles Choice

The fundamental choice in strategy is whether to go alone, or to cooperate with others. Going alone may allow the entity to keep

---

[10]Ironically, too large an opportunity often causes the entity to overextend itself and fail or die.

[11]These single-celled animals have a remarkable ability (as a group) to find food through a human-constructed maze, and then share the delivery of this food to all parts of the group.

all the rewards for himself, but also involve going long stretches without any wins. Going with a group reduces the risk of long stretches of starvation, but then the entity has to share everything, and essentially cannot do much better than the other members of the group.

Going alone allows the entity to pivot strategies faster, particularly in situations that have an immediate issue to be addressed. However going alone can also lead to more volatility in outcomes compared to going with a group or herd where pivoting strategies requires more coordination and communication. Working as a group may help in the diversity of experience and strategies available to use in a particular context, but imposes the additional cost of coordinating some form of agreement.

The ancient Greek anecdote related to this dilemma concerns Achilles, the greatest warrior of his time. Before his birth he was asked to choose between a short and eventful life and a long and uneventful life. He chose the eventful one. It is implied in the tale that each of us is also given the choice, and that most of us choose the long life, and hence give up any chance at fame or fortune.

The strategic choice for any entity in the face of uncertainty and competition is similar to what Achilles faced. Do I go alone and keep the rewards for myself, or do I cooperate with others and live a long life with no individual glory?

Why does Achilles Choice talk only about two alternatives? Achilles was not an ordinary warrior. He was the best (or destined to be the best, when he was offered this choice). He won many battles. Yet, at the end of each he probably had a choice- to continue on this lone warrior strategy, or to be part of the group. An ordinary soldier may well have a short and uneventful life. This does not apply to Achilles.

Consider the eventful life. The events we are talking about are, of course, battles and fights. No matter how good a warrior you are, the odds are usually against you in any individual battle. Once you consider a series of battles, the odds catch up with you rather fast. The eventful life cannot be long.

Fighting alone brings fame and recognition. While it lasts.

4.3.4 The Basis of Organizations

Some entities choose a long and uneventful life over a short and eventful life[12]. On the one hand, there is the small probability of making large gains in a long stretch of time when they make no gains at all. On the other hand there is the larger probability of more frequent and predictable (smaller) gains over their lifetime when working with a group. These entities choose the latter.

They choose to be part of a group. We shall call these groups organizations in a broad sense of the term.

Any loss in motivation for entities (from the smaller rewards or lower risks) is presumably compensated by various other benefits from organizing. For example, the organization may be much more efficient in gathering resources compared with the lone entity. We will describe the organization over the next section and subsequent chapters.

4.4 Defining the Organization

What is an organization? We can break this down into smaller questions in this way

- How do entities know what is an organization? For example, how do hunters determine membership in the group?

- Are there rules which allow for the incorporation of new members, or the expulsion of existing members?

- What does the optimal group size depend upon?

- How does the communication methods/technology used by members determine the group size?

- How is the optimal group size determined by the resources dedicated to inter-group details (or, how is pack size determined by the size of a primate's brain)?

---

[12]Not all entities need to choose to live long and uneventful lives. This may depend upon how resource-rich the environment is, how skillful the entity is, how experienced the entity is, and a host of other random factors.

- How does group efficiency increase or decrease with pack or organization size?

We may ask similar questions of the human body, which is an organization composed of billions of single cells. We may also ask the same of Walmart, composed of tens of thousands of employees.

Even a simple group of entities like a pack of wolves has many social norms that each member/wolf follows. When do they learn the rules? Perhaps some of these are hard coded in their DNA, and perhaps some more are learned when socializing with other cubs. There is a pecking order. Sharing each kill does not mean that the share is equal for all wolves. This may be unequal in quantity, or it may be unequal in quality, with the leader getting the first pick. In some cases being closer to the top of the pecking order is its own reward.

Using numerous examples from different layers we see that organizations are collections of entities that have decided to cooperate, but have also developed many behavior patterns to ensure that the organization itself functions well. The nature of organizations is similar, whether we are studying cells or communities. We seek to find out what drives the similarity in their nature across such different layers.

4.4.1 Members

The first item an organization needs is a definition of membership.

An organization cannot practically encompass all entities at every level. There has to be a real or virtual boundary that informs everyone that those inside are members, and those outside are non-members[13]. The basis for membership has to be some physical, behavioral or virtual attributes that are stable in the short run, and which allow members to identify each other and accept or reject them[14].

---

[13]We will later discuss different nuances of membership.

[14]Some researchers have observed that the average number of social interpersonal relationships that one human being can grasp is a bit larger than 200. Thus, "flat" human social organizations like neighborhood organizations

Members may identify each other with easily observable attributes like plumage and coloring, size and shape, smell and pheromones, and many other sensory details. Some membership attributes may be genetic, which means that membership is determined at birth and cannot be changed afterwards. Sparrows of a particular flock may have some attributes which are common-these attributes form the "rules" of membership. A sparrow cannot become a crow.

Some membership attributes can come through familiarity and proximity, which means that membership is not determined by DNA or birth. A wolf may have a choice of packs to join.

Membership by behavior complements membership by attribute. There are many species of birds where the main form of differentiation are the details of the song and the courtship dance by each species. In many cases the intensity of differentiation is higher the more similar these attributes or behaviors are.

For example, one could argue that compared to all human beings, the members in different professional basketball teams are actually almost identical. They are in a much narrower range of physical attributes like height, weight, bone density, physical response times and body fat percent. They are also very similar in terms of life experiences, like hours of practice each day, participation in high school and college teams. Yet the intensity of identification and differentiation is higher the more similar the teams are, or the closer they reside, or the more equal the past

---

tend to gravitate towards that size, and may also tend to split up if they get much larger. We mention "flat" since it is possible to aggregate community organizations by creating a membership hierarchy, the way medieval armies may have been organized. Early management research also focused on the concept of span of control, which attempts to find out the ideal number of subordinates a manager/supervisor could effectively coordinate. Each of those subordinates could, in turn, be a supervisor for more individuals. Thus, even before the advent of communication technology like horses and telegraphs, it was possible to build up rather large hierarchical organizations. An interesting effect of better communication and information technologies has been the ability to "flatten" the organization by removing some layers of middle management whose purpose was to enable top-bottom communication in both directions.

record has been.

Entities spend a lot of time, effort and resources to maintain their membership, and to evaluate others on their membership.

4.4.2 Outside the Organization

Once we have an organization, we can define "us" and we can define "them". In proto-organizations the division between us and them develops over time. Some members may participate in some of the activities of the organization and follow some of the rules, but not all. Some members may drop in and out of the organization as is convenient for them.

Organizations may have core members and affiliate members, which attempts to formalize differential membership. Thus, in various ways, membership may also end up as a continuum. Members reside at different distances from the central mission and purpose. Those who are close to the central premise often cannot conceive of a world without that core, while those who are furthest in this continuum can also see other viewpoints.

This also leads to the existence of entities that cannot belong to the organization, but who are useful to the organization, and complement its activities in different ways. These may be called symbiotes for the specific organization, and the mutually beneficial relationship between the organization and this helpful entity is called symbiosis[15].

A symbiote may act as a buffer between the organization and other organizations or other entities. They may also provide services that the entities belonging to the organization cannot or will not do, perhaps since they contradict some of the rules or principles necessary to organizational membership.

The emergence of an organization may cause a group of cooperating entities to be divided across the boundary of the organization. Some of them are "inside" and some "outside". Although they may continue to engage in the common activity, now they are

---

[15]In this discussion we will consider those symbiotes which are entities themselves, rather than other symbiotic organizations.

separated by membership. This may lead to complete separation, where they no longer cooperate, or it may lead to a symbiotic relationship where they may still work together albeit unequally.

There is more that exists outside the organization than just symbiotes. This will be revisited in Chapter 7 where we will again discuss symbiotes, as well as scavengers and predators.

4.4.3 Dead Ends

The emergence of an organization does not mean that every entity is swept up into that organization. Every molecule does not become part of a macro molecule, every macro molecule does not become part of a cell, and every cell does not join or create a multi-cellular organization. Thus, the world has many entities that are free-floating, and continue to be so over time. There are also entities that actively resist the creation of organizations because they do not accept the rules.

These entities may believe in their own ability to survive, or they may have enough foresight to realize that the potential emergence of organizations will reorder the winners and losers to their detriment. Thus, they "play dirty" and hurt other entities in competitions and similarly actively thwart the creation of organizations in other manners. This also means that in case any organizations do arise, the rule breakers are intrinsically incapable of creating or maintaining stable organizations. Even if more than one organization arises, these entities do not join any of them, even when they can.

Viruses are examples of large-molecule rule breakers. They break the rules by attacking and destroying cells to reproduce and create more copies of themselves. However, before the emergence of cells and cellular boundaries there was no way of labeling a virus as a rule breaker, since there were no rules to break. Perhaps at that time there were many such half-organizations that were more complex than large molecules, but less complex than cells. Some of these entities evolved over generations to become cells, while others stayed as viruses. After all, at the level of molecular interactions a virus does not do anything differently from other cells.

Similarly, pathogenic bacteria are cellular rule breakers, since they attack multi-cellular organizations and may sometimes destroy them. However, they have existed even before multi-cellular organizations came into being. Thus pathogenic bacteria started "breaking rules" only after multi-cellular organizations came into existence, along with their book of rules.

Viruses, bacteria and similar examples in the other layers have existed for a long time, but they have not created a parallel branch of organizations. They prefer to be anti-organizational, and will continue to be so as long as life exists.

These are organizational dead ends. Viruses did not go on to create living cells. Bacteria continue to exist as single entities while many other cells have evolved into multi-cellular creatures.

4.4.4   Organizational Overhead

The membership identification process carries with it a cost, a cognitive and enforcement overhead. This does not contribute much towards procurement of resources, but is focused exclusively on determining and enforcing membership.

If the membership attributes are sensory, then clearly these senses and the brainpower behind the senses must be capable of differentiating the variations in these attributes across the many entities, and then deciding whether they are in-group or out-of-group.

Within our bodies there is a complex mechanism which determines whether a particular cell is a member or not, and the body may kill or reject cells which it has identified as non-members. This can happen as designed during blood transfusions and organ transplants, which is why we use immune system suppressing drugs. It can also happen incorrectly in various auto-immune diseases when these mechanisms incorrectly identify parts of one's own body as non-members and start attacking them.

For the bird this involves devoting large parts of the brain towards remembering and differentiating songs and dances. When does a bird learn this? Is this encoded in their DNA, or is it triggered by specific patterns of movements of its parent birds when the fledgling is in the nest? Either way, the bird brain is pushed to its limit in discerning species and flock membership.

If the membership is behavioral, then the entity itself must also devote resources to learning and executing the specific behavior. Is this person a fan of a specific sports team? Just buying the jersey is not enough. She must also celebrate every team win, and know the chants that are hurled at opposing teams.

For large organizations there may be specific sub-organizations devoted to enforcing norms and attributes. Many religions have groups of religious police, particularly in times of social change and upheaval. Groups of auditors from large auto companies often visit suppliers and retailers to ensure that their facilities and processes are in compliance and there is no impact on the brand and reputation of the auto company. Membership and enforcement is an integral part of the existence of all organizations, particularly those with a large membership[16].

Thus, organizations arise since they reduce uncertainty and risk for entities. We will now explore a critical aspect of life inside the organization- in-system competition.

---

[16]Enforcing membership can often take on a life of its own separate from the original motivation for the creation of the organization.

Chapter 5

Competition as Art

In this chapter we will explore why most of the competition we see in the universe is actually art, and what that means for the entity. We will define art in a broader sense as well.

We have already seen that the organization exists because its members chose to unite as an outcome of their desire to live a long and uneventful life. But that does not reduce or remove the need to compete.

Here lies the paradox of organizations. On the one hand entities in an organization have decided that they must collaborate-otherwise the risk of death is too high. On the other hand, they still have to figure out some way of establishing a hierarchy and defining "winners" and "losers" in some way that mimics the life they have chosen to give up.

This is addressed by setting up artificial competitions with well-defined rules that are periodically conducted inside the organization.

As you read this chapter some questions you may apply to your context are:

- What is the main type of competition that the entities engage in within the organization?

- To what extent do the skills developed for such competitions translate to tasks with concrete functional benefits like the procurement of food and other resources?

- What are the concrete benefits that an entity gets from winning such a competition? What are the additional social benefits of winning? Which type of benefit is larger?

- What are the rules of the competition that ensure a degree of parity across competing entities inside the organization?

The main concepts covered in this chapter are highlighted in Figure 5.1. All of them arise from the existence of organizations.

5.1 Inside the Organization

The core motivation for some entities getting together and forming an alliance or organization of any type is their preference for a longer and less stressful life over a shorter and more eventful one. This does not eliminate the equally fundamental need for all entities to compete. No organization, whether built on a chemical, biological, social or political framework, can continue if it ignores the basic nature of its entities. The need to compete and/or grow is the prime directive, and this drives a successful entity to expand into and fill up whatever new opportunity or niche it may discover. Joining an organization creates a fundamental tension between the innate need to compete and grow and the need to cooperate. There is always the temptation to push or break the implicit or explicit rules and norms of the organization related to sharing the spoils each day.

Every entity that joins an organization realizes that the benefits of sharing are far better than going alone- it may get hurt and die in direct conflict, or it may starve to death. The need to compete is equally strong. The core reason to join the organization is the implicit promise of no death, or a lower probability of death, either from direct competition, or from hunger.

How do we resolve this tension between two opposite directives?

It may sound simple- we must compete, but we cannot kill or hurt another. This leads to the creation of a specialized type of competition that we can call in-system competition. In contrast,

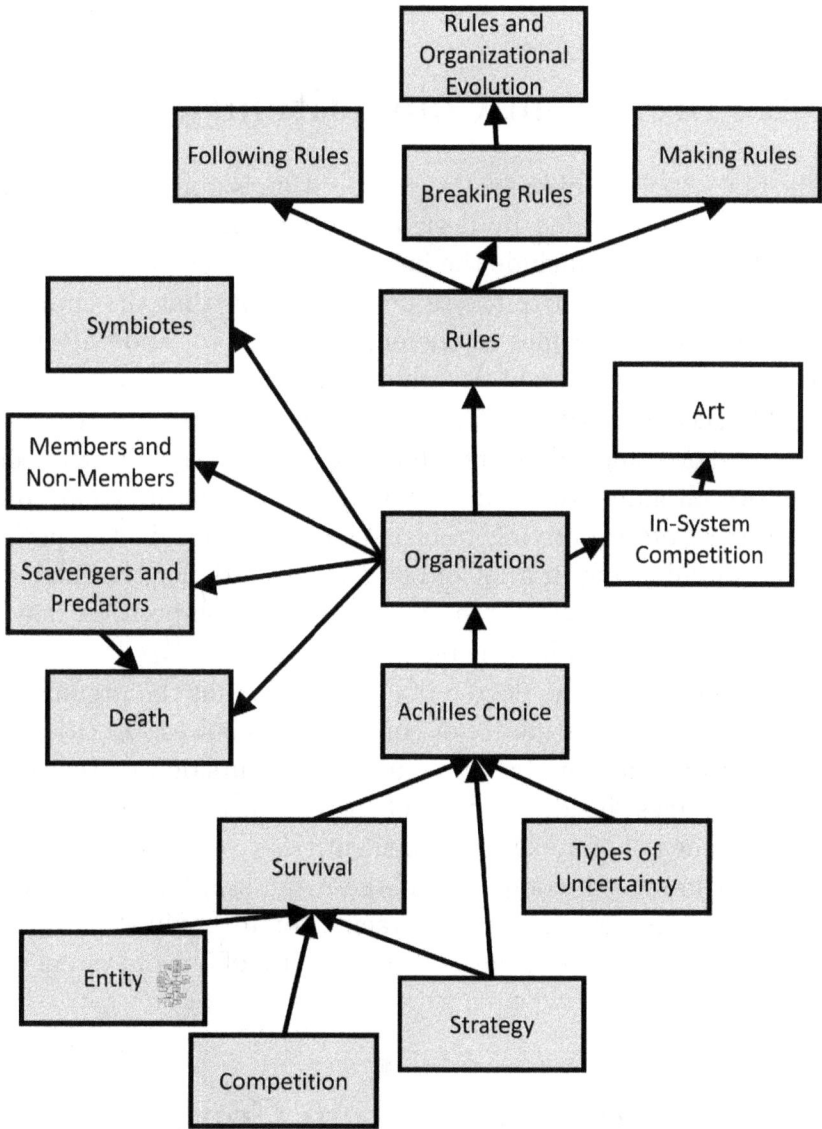

Figure 5.1: Chapter 5 Map: Members, Non-Members and Art

the type of competition we have been describing thus far can be called out-of-system competition, the brutal type, with death on the cards.

5.2   In-System Competition

The first attribute of in-system competition is quite simple. Death is explicitly forbidden by design. In this context, death can be broadened to also include the inability to participate, rather than "physical" death. There has to be a guarantee that the entity can compete as many times as the entity wishes to, and withdrawal from competition should be voluntary.

The second attribute of in-system competition is that the award is often something quite non-functional, like a small metal cup. The overall gains from winning in-system competitions are often quite real, often deriving from a higher position in the pecking order, culminating in a lot of concrete rewards for the final winner. Since all entities wish to compete, a competition may be vicariously followed by others.

Depending on the degree of cohesion within the organization there may be a continuum of competition choices. Entities may choose from the raw, brutal competition "outside", or the highly stylized games "inside". A part of the organization has to be subject to some risk, for example when entities go out to hunt for food. In many in-system competitions there can still be the accidental near-death, for example in car racing, or in boxing. Accidental injuries remind entities of the brutal nature of out-of-system competition.

5.3   Parity in In-System Competition

Consider an out-of-system competitive scenario. This is difficult, since almost all vertebrates, social or otherwise, have evolved to have very stylized rules of interaction, even across species. Nevertheless, take the hypothetical situation where an individual is accosted by a mean mugger with a knife in a dark alley. This "engagement" does not last very long.

On the other hand, consider an in-system competition, perhaps when two sports teams meet on the field, or when two males face off in a herd. That can continue for hours.

In-system competition favors a parity among competitors, since otherwise it is difficult to sustain the intensity and credibility of long competitions. There are weight classes in sports ranging from boxing to weight-lifting. It would be "unfair" to have boxers, for example, compete across weight classes. In many team sports leagues the teams choose from the new crop of players in reverse order- the team ranked at the bottom of the league in the previous year gets to pick first.

Any disparity among competitors obviously favors the better-endowed competitor in the short run, but hurts the competition and hence all competitors in the long run. It is extremely boring if the same entity wins every time[1].

Thus, arbitrary rules arise over time to ensure that no single entity can capture all the spoils of an in-system competition, whether in one round or over multiple rounds. The competitive uncertainty about survival is mostly replaced with the uncertainty over which entity will win. In-system competition cannot eliminate all competitive elements. That would be boring. There is little interest in seeing a large wrestler take on a small one. On the other hand there is slightly more interest in seeing two wrestlers of the same size, and definitely more interest if this size is at the larger end of the scale.

Non-human in-system competition is everywhere around us. Consider two young males from a herd facing off of each other to establish herd hierarchy. Even a small probability of injury or death every time this happened would dramatically weaken the herd and the species. Thus, every in-species competition is an example of in-system competition. Fiddler crabs, deer, bison, birds, humans comparing muscle cars, all of these are examples

---

[1]We will not talk here about competition among the competitions- that is what is happens in many cases. We close the loop later in Chapter 6.

of in-system competition. Perhaps bacteria, who have means of chemical signaling, also back off hunting a target if it can be identified as kin.

5.4 Functionality and Art

Functionality has a simple definition: it helps the physical process of living. Food, clothes and basic housing all have functional benefits. On the other hand, a certificate for winning a chess tournament against other humans has no immediate primary functional benefit for the winning human.

There are certainly a lot of functional-skill-based in-system competitions. Boxing and wrestling are definitely skills that may help if under any condition a human had to fight another human in an out-of-system competition. Over time, almost anything can become a dimension of in-system competition. Consider running, which is functionally one step removed from wrestling. One can come up with scenarios where running a hundred meters faster than others by one hundredth of a second has functional benefits, but we are probably stretching the likelihood of seeing such a scenario play out in real life. Yet running is one of the most coveted in-system competitions, particularly the short distances.

Restricting in-system competitions to functional skills will leave out the majority of entities. In fact, most entities will never be the fastest, strongest, or cleverest of their species even in their own communities. Yet they have the need to compete too.

Thus, the majority of competitions among entities end up taking place in a dimension that has little or no functional benefit. Yet even for these competitions the competitive element is real. Even though there is no injury or death involved, the actual competition involves skills that will take a long time and a lot of commitment to develop. Often the rules themselves are complex and require understanding. Many in-system competitions are cognitive, sometimes with echoes of functional benefits.

If an entity loses a competition, then there is no death, injury or functional impairment- unless one counts disappointment and depression (which are real indeed). The entity is free to pick up the pieces, work on skill improvement, and then enter the next round. Even if the entity wins, the actual payoff may be a certificate or cup of not particular functional value.

Often any functional prizes like cash awards are rarely enough to pay for all the individual investment of time and effort leading up to the competition. It may, at most, bring a big payoff to an extremely small number of entities. It certainly does not cover the time and effort invested by all the competitors as a group. The competition is certain to see negative returns to the organization as a whole.

5.5   Examples of Art

Many athletes practice running an arbitrary distance of 26.2 miles called a marathon. They commit years of their youth and depend upon family or sponsors during this time to improve their performance to competitive levels. The races do not involve life-or-death risks, but still carry rewards derived from the community of runners who want to run similarly. The chances of getting direct functional benefit from being able to run the marathon are disproportionately smaller than the resources needed to develop this capability at competitive levels. However, the rewards from winning the marathon at the Olympics carries some very real rewards.

Each year there are more than a million high school starters in the US in any specific sport. That number drops down to a couple of thousand each year at the college level, only a fraction of whom are on a sports scholarship. Out of these a few dozen make it to the draft and enter professional sports, if indeed a league exists for that sport. Most of these players have professional careers lasting less than ten years. There is just about one professional player in a decade who breaks out and is known by people who are not interested in the sport to begin with. Even with this bleak payoff scenario, there are often other indirect benefits in terms of community. It may help the entity find a mate, a profession, perhaps reputation and stature in the community.

While not as elaborate as a national championship or the Olympics, in-system competitions exist in non-human species as well. This is often related to signaling and submission. For every video of two bucks rushing at each other and butting heads, there are numerous instances of them facing off for a long time, with one of the bucks backing off only after hours of competition. For each one of the face offs there are many more outcomes that are determined earlier in the nursery in the course of rough play.

Male deer commit significant physiological resources towards the development of multi-point antlers. It is no mean feat, and requires a significant effort. These formidable weapons are almost never used to hurt another contender for the top buck position in the herd. Deer conflict usually takes the form of long, staring matches with one contender eventually submitting without a fight. They rarely even come to the head-butt that is usually shown on nature documentaries. Death is extremely rare.

But the foraging and reproductive rewards from this stylized conflict are quite real. The antler is dual-purpose. Though it deliberately confers no benefit for in-system competitions, it can be used as a defensive weapon against predators. This makes it even more remarkable, since the entity is aware of the lethality of the antlers as weapons, but never uses them in-system.

There are other examples where the functional aspect is not very clear. The male in a particular bird species prepares a nest of blue stones and other blue objects to attract females. This is, again, not trivial. Perhaps this is an evolution from certain species where the male brings a gift of food for the female. Perhaps in contexts of abundance that functional task was no longer adequate as a competitive dimension, and some random confluence of factors led to stones replacing food. Why blue? Perhaps because blue was an important color in the environment and the species is able to differentiate shades of blue. Why does a specific female choose a blue stone arrangement by one male rather than the other? Perhaps there is someone who is currently gathering data to answer these questions. Perhaps we shall never know.

Are there systems in which these rules are broken? Do systems exist in which the "bucks" do gore each other to death, so that there is actually only one male in each herd? Death or injury is counter to the core reason for joining the herd. If the bucks can be potentially aggressive, then the adults can probably be even more so. There are species where any adolescent males must leave the herd or risk death from the single alpha male. Interestingly, such species are frequently apex predators, and do not have to worry about injury from other species in the normal course of events.

As we have already seen, many entities engage in competitive activities that have no direct functional benefit, e.g. male birds collecting blue stones around the nest, various human sporting competitions, or other ritualized activities. These activities require significant commitment of time and resources in order to achieve mastery, and are often appreciated by other entities on the strength of written rules or unwritten norms.

Thus, in-system competition is artistic in nature. In-system competition has been there before primates came onto the scene, and shall continue to play an important role in all organizations.

Does that mean that human art is competitive in nature too? The human definition of art encompasses various fields of entertainment and expression. We have solitary artistic activities like painting, writing, composing music and others. Each of these artistic activities can be collaborative as well. We also have a whole host of performing arts, from music, dance, theater, improvisational performances and others. In many ways these are indirectly competitive since there are some artists who are more popular than others, and this competition is in-system- each artist can continue to create/perform as long as he/she desires.

All artists have at different times battled with the motivation behind their creativity. Are they doing this for internal self-actualization or for external recognition and rewards? They have also battled their own diversion of their artistic desire due to the temptations of external rewards (hence the term "selling out").

It is also interesting to note that the aggregation of artists into organizations and schools is a very common phenomenon, and it is only the rare artist who can transcend the context from which they have arisen.

Any kind of art can be competitive, and all in-system competition has elements of art. A sportsman executing a new or daring strategy to better an opponent, an animation artist rendering a scene in a new way, a whale singing a new song: all of these are as intensely artistic as they are competitive.

Chapter 6

Following and Modifying Rules

In this chapter we will dig deeper into the nature of rules. Every organization has rules. Indeed, that is the basis of any organization. These rules may be explicit or implicit. They may be encoded in the entity's genetic code, in the wiring of its brain, or trained into children at an early age. As the organization becomes more structured and defined, many explicit rules, implicit norms and other patterns emerge.

Before the organization comes into existence and a rule is defined there can be no rule breakers. It is the emergence of the "rule" of private property that also defines the thief. It is the emergence of formal roads that gives birth to wrong-way driving. It is the emergence of society that gives rise to a legal drinking age. It is the emergence of multi-cellular organizations that defines cancer.

Some of the questions you can ask about the rules that may be applicable to your context are:

- What is the length and complexity of the explicit rules that all members are expected to follow? How many of these have compliance enforcement mechanisms (like police), and governance processes (like courts or appeals processes)?

- What is the degree of voluntary compliance of each rule?

What is the compliance enforcement cost for each rule?

- Who are the primary rule-breakers in the organization? Does the fraction and frequency of rule-breaking increase with the "status" or "importance" of the member?

- How does the organization review and change rules? What fraction of members participate in the rule-modification process?

- How does the rule-modification process drive the change and evolution of the organization?

The primary concepts covered in this chapter are shown in Figure 6.1. Following rules, breaking rules or making them can only exist inside an organization.

6.1   Following Rules

As the entities in an organization spend more time together, they create rules to codify existing norms, since there is a natural variance among entities in their understanding and following of these norms.

There is no need to create a rule stating that all humans must breathe air, at least until genetic modifications allow us to breathe something else in its place. There is also no confusion about whether an entity is a human or a fish, since they belong to different organizations (if they do indeed affiliate themselves to any organization). On the other hand, we need many rules to decide who is a fan of a specific sports team.

It is practically impossible to monitor and ensure compliance for all rules all the time. Even if the cost of monitoring decreases due to technological advancements, the cost of ensuring compliance still exists.

It is certainly tempting to attempt complete enforcement of all rules. In the human context many organizations and political systems have attempted to do so, at great cost to both the

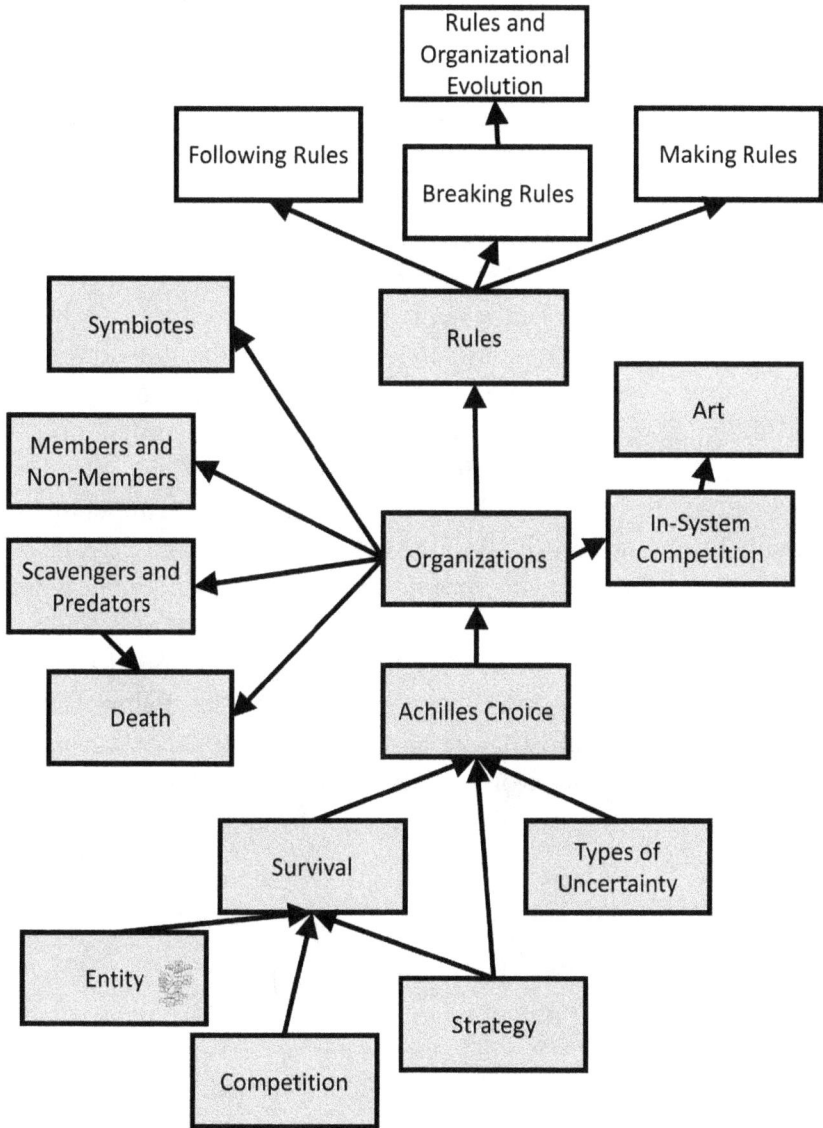

Figure 6.1: Chapter 6 Map: Following, Breaking and Making Rules

enforcers and the enforcees. Why should there be a need to enforce compliance at such cost? If indeed the difference is too wide perhaps there should be two organizations. This happens quite frequently (evolutionarily speaking) in causing the divergence of one group of entities from one species into two. In a large flock of birds perhaps their mating rituals diverge, or perhaps it is their plumage.

In most organizations the punishment options for a rule-breaker are usually a variation of revocation of membership and a decreasing access to the community and resources that the membership allows. This is sometimes contradictory to the need to have an egalitarian organization. Ideally, there is both uniformity in compliance to the organization's rules as well as a separation between the ability and willingness to comply between members and non-members (hence a clear organizational boundary).

If a rule is frequently broken, then either the rule changes to reflect the changes in the population of entities in an organization, or some entities leave the organization- individually or in a group.

In every organization there are always people who follow the rules because that is what they have been conditioned to do. On the other hand some more experienced entities follow the rules since they understand the purpose of rules and hence have a more nuanced view of the world. This may often happen after they have broken a few rules and learned from the consequences of their actions.

6.2   Breaking Rules

Rules cannot exist without rule breakers. After all, what is the purpose of a rule if nobody ever breaks it. (At this point we are discussing entities who break the rules within an organization, not predators.)

There are different kinds of rule breakers within an organization. The largest dichotomy is between ignorant rule breakers who usually do not know that they are breaking rules, and conscious rule breakers who know that they are doing so. Ignorant rule breakers are usually forgiven, no matter how irritating they are to the usual scheme of things, while conscious rule breakers may or may not be punished.

Let us examine the types of rule breakers, with the caveat that this is almost certainly an incomplete list of categories.

6.2.1 Children

"Children" are assumed to have incomplete knowledge and comprehension of rules, and hence are given a large leeway in their violations of rules. For example, even though it is socially unacceptable to pee in public, very young children are not censured for accidentally doing so. By the time they are three years old, however, it is commonly expected that they will have much less frequent accidents. Similarly, a graduate in a first job may spend many months figuring out the social rules around work, attendance, lunch and inter-departmental relations after she joins a firm. Any violations are usually assumed to be due to ignorance.

6.2.2 Visitors

"Visitors" are capable of following rules, but they may often break rules because the rules are different in a new context. Tourists often dress inappropriately when they visit other countries. A manager visiting a different country is often ignorant of the cultural norms around gifting, exchanging business cards, or how organizational hierarchy impacts the order of introduction.

Visitors are irritating when they make mistakes, and their old habits acquired in a home location can take a long time to unlearn in a new context. If they are visiting for a short time, then the hosts may often make no effort to change the visitor's behavior. If such visitors occur frequently, then the rude and irritating behavior may be accepted as the new norm for this specific context.

The next few types of rule breakers are conscious rule breakers-they know the rules, and break them deliberately. How an organization deals with conscious rule breakers is also different.

6.2.3 Marginal Rule-Breakers

"Marginal rule-breakers" are a natural consequence of the dispersion of rule compliance among entities. Pick any rule, and you will immediately find marginal rule-breakers, depending upon the intensity of enforcement. We have all broken some rules on the margin: driving a few miles above the speed limit, coming a few minutes late to meetings, and so on.

6.2.4 Teenagers

"Teenagers" are entities who rebel and act out against the rules when they learn and comprehend them. Perhaps this is motivated by rebellion against increasing restrictions as they grow up from the relative freedom of childhood. Perhaps this is driven by an innate drive to try out different rules. There is always a tension between the socialization of children into existing rules and norms, and the need to discover new forms of the rules and norms.

6.2.5 Central Rule-Breakers

"Central rule-breakers" are the most complex and the rarest of rule breakers. This is not your common garden variety rule breaker. This is an entity which breaks the rules after a long life in the core of the system, one who knows all the rules, and knows the ramifications of breaking any specific rule. A central rule-breaker has had success working with the rules of the organization, and then uses deep insights to break the rules in a fundamental manner.

With each incident of conscious rule-breaking a vaguely specified norm moves towards a clearer definition. This also accelerates the move towards the codification of norms into rules, and a forced separation of entities along the continuum of rule acceptance. Thus, each rule draws more clearly the boundary of the organization. During this phase the symbiotes initially left out of the organization are grudgingly accepted for their indispensability in doing essential tasks that the organizational entities will not do.

6.3   Organizational Variations

An organization is possible when the environment allows for some rewards to be gained by opportunity-seeking entities which co-operate. Each organization is the result of the need to reduce operating uncertainty among these entities. Once a successful organizational structure has been discovered it is then replicated until the entire expanse has been exploited. After the initial random discovery of this best-working-solution the focus of the organization changes to replication with minor variations. The successful organization is often blind to everything else except the execution of the strategy that it was created to embody.

However the environment changes over time, often due to the existence and spread of this solution itself. If all that the organization does is to replicate itself to follow the rules exactly, then after a while (measured in life generations of the organization), all copies of the organization will perish since the original opportunity may have changed or disappeared. Thus, over time any organization that figures out ways to experiment with its strategy when creating copies of itself will be better suited to variations in the environment.

Since many of the rules of the organization are arbitrary, there are two ways in which strategy variations can be uncovered within the life of the organization (a) teenagers and (b) central rule break-ers.

Teenagers reject the rules when they learn more about them at the end of childhood. Some of them may then start on the process of reinventing these rules by trial-and-error for themselves.

Central rule-breakers work at the other end of the spectrum, usually after finishing a long stint in leadership. They spend a long period of their life following all the rules, which gives them a comprehensive understanding of the interactions of the parts of the system. This may allow them to significantly modify multiple rules. These changes may still be accepted by a majority of the entities, and result in a smoother transition from one strategy to another.

Thus, central-rule-breakers may be the fastest way to change to a strategy that is demonstrably better for a changed observable environment. On the other hand, teenagers are a better hedge against a radically changed environment where organizations have to be rebuilt from the ground up.

6.4 Us and Them

If there is no organization or system, then there are no rules that have been defined, and hence there are no rule-breakers. There may be an awareness of what rules could be created in order to make the world "a better place for everyone". However, an awareness of potential rules does not automatically translate to a path to the actualization of these rules.

A defined organizational boundary helps to separate us from them. We are good, and they are bad. We live in peace, and they are the barbarians. We are saved, and they are heathens. We are rational, and they are stupid.

Deeply embedded members are the engine and the core of the organization. Most of them are ignorant about the complete range of the organization's activities. They are generally unable to comprehend life outside the organization. Thus, entities deep inside the organization are also the most unconscious rule-followers. As we choose entities further away from the center of the organization, the entities are more aware of the potential to violate rules, but usually still choose to follow the rules. Thus, in general, the further away from the center we travel the higher the consciousness of the rule-followers.

At the boundary, an entity is almost indifferent to the benefits and costs of belonging to the organization. Perhaps life in the wild is, on the balance, just as attractive as life in the fold. Perhaps there is no wild, only competing organizations, and at best a symbiotic relationship with one of the organizations already crowding the landscape.

Every organization needs a management or leadership structure if it needs to grow beyond a small number of members. Since this is usually built from the core or deeply embedded members, there had to be some mechanism by which there is awareness of the difference between the internal world of the organization and the external world outside its boundaries. A leadership which is ignorant of the nature of the organization it leads and the role that various rule-breakers play can move towards enforcing rules in a severe way. This drives out the marginal members and weakens the organization.

6.5   Recursion, or Back to the Beginning

This brings us back to the start of the process. We started by assuming that certain entities exist, and then explored the motivation behind the creation of organizations. Now we are at a point where a successful organization has replicated to fill up a niche, and hence needs to complete against other organizations for resources.

The resources that an organization needs to survive and grow are, of course, different from the resources that the entities needed. However, the parallels are quite clear. Hence, these organizations can now be considered entities in their own right, and we start the process of figuring out the game all over again.

Chapter 7

Asymmetric Competition

Standard (or symmetric) competition is the battle for resources between members in the same layer. Asymmetric competition, on the other hand, is the battle for resources between entities that exist across layers.

When we consider human beings, for example, we are not only competing or cooperating with other human beings, we are also competing with other cells that do not share our specific DNA. Similarly, each of our cells is not just competing or cooperating with other cells, they are also competing with other molecules that do not belong to a specific cell. At every layer the very existence of the being is a temporary truce across the multiple battles within each layer, and also across layers

For your context, consider the following questions

- Consider members who are not part of your organization. What role do they play?

- How stable are groups of members in the organization, particularly when the organization dies? What are the components of a deceased organization that can be re-used by other organizations? Do organizations exist who swiftly reuse the members and member groups of an organization that has broken up due to other reasons?

- Is there a clear divide between different organizations that are composed of similar members along the lines of predator and prey? In other words, are there organizations whose sole mode of sustenance is to attack other organizations with the intent of consuming or assimilating their members?

- Is the battle between these two groups of organizations an arms race of ever increasing tactics and countermeasures? How has this played out over time?

- Finally, are there non-member entities that live around the boundary of the organization (both inside and outside) who "help out" the organization in important tasks that the organization cannot or will not do?

The concepts of asymmetric competition that will be covered in this chapter are shown in Figure 7.1. Scavengers, Predators and Symbiotes can be explained only through the process of asymmetric competition.

7.1   Introduction

Asymmetric competition occurs between entities that are not similar in some way. The continuum of such competition can be summarized in three types of entities: scavengers, predators and symbiotes.

When we were considering out-of-system competition between similar entities, we accounted for the possibility of injury and death, but it was assumed that if one entity did die, that was the end of the story. In asymmetric competition, that is not the end of the story. After all, the dead entity still retains a degree of organization at the lower levels, which is valuable.

Are scavengers and predators breaking rules? It is not immediately clear which rules they are breaking. Scavengers and the others are not simple rule-breaking entities. To incorporate scavengers we have to start at a different point, rather than the obvious stereotypes of, say lions and deer.

Predatory behavior cannot be defined as (symmetric) competition between similar entities for the current level. To understand this we have to start at the next lower level, i.e. as

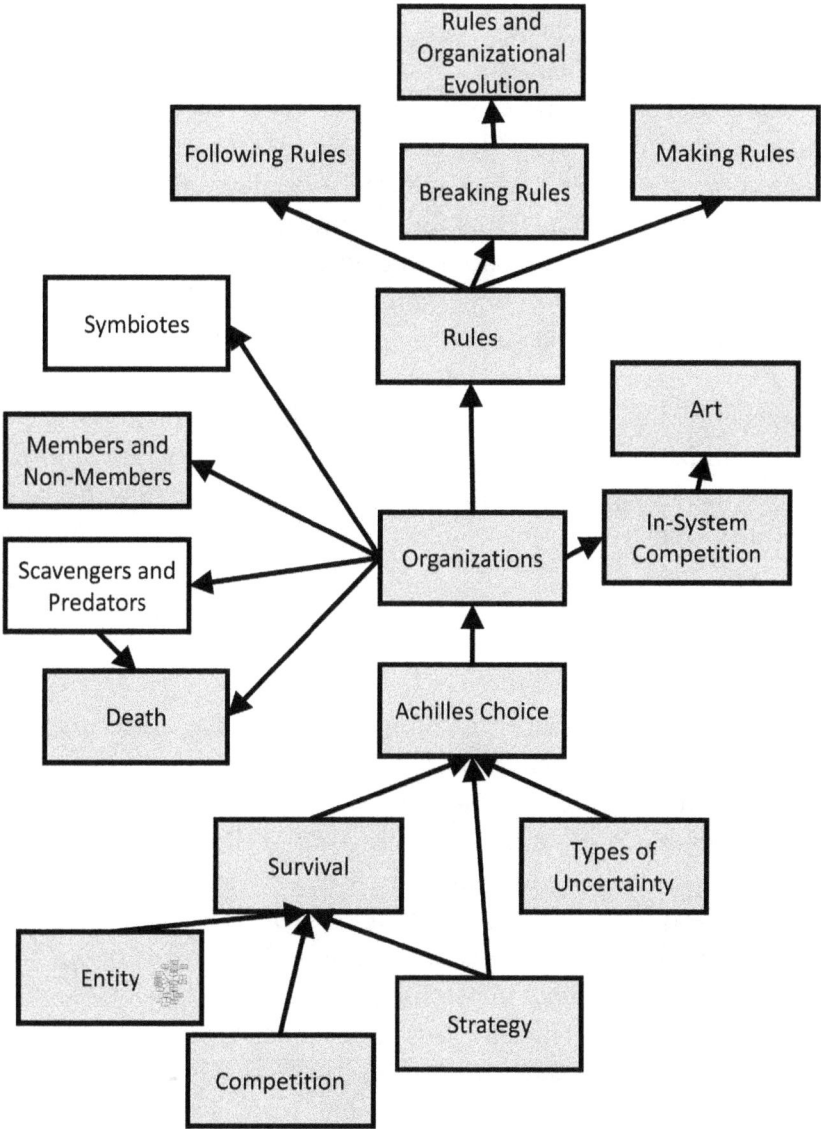

Figure 7.1: Chapter 7 Map: Asymmetric Competition

(asymmetric) competition between different organizations since they both need the common member entities. At the level just below both the predator and the prey, similar entities make up both of them. Predators hunt prey precisely because prey have similar constituent entities.

Consider an environment full of entities before stable organizations have come into existence. For example, let us say that there are lots of replicating macro-molecules, but we do not yet have stable cells. Thus, unstable organizations form and dissolve quite frequently. At this point the entities are quite freely mobile, and an entity may join one organization to begin with, and then find another organization when the first one dissolves.

Proto-scavenger organizations form under these circumstances. Scavengers are organizations that reuse bits and pieces of the earlier organizations. The smallest bit of an old organization is, of course, an entity. But there may be slightly larger reusable pieces, even working groups that can form a part of the next organization.

7.2 Scavengers

Thus, the earliest instances of re-usability of a structure comes from scavengers scooping up parts of recently "deceased" organizations, rather than from genetic code which an organization may use to create a copy of itself. There are benefits to the scavengers, of course, in reusing existing forms of entities. There are benefits to these forms as well, and those groups of entities that can survive the longest after the dissolution of the older organization also have an advantage in getting picked up by the new one. They may even be more efficient in doing the activities they are tasked with, which makes them attractive to the scavengers as well.

It may be difficult to define when an unstable organization dissolves. There will be situations where an organization cycles between formation and dissolution many times. Under these circumstances exactly when a scavenger crosses the line and turns into a predator may also be hard to define.

When stable organizations arise after many cycles of unstable organizations, then the line between scavengers and predators is also clear. Scavengers use the parts from a dissolved organization, and predators use the components from a viable organization. Thus, predators are also defined precisely only when an organization becomes stable. Predators, after all, necessarily use the same entities as the prey.

7.3   Predators

Once we have a clear and stable organization, we can distinguish between scavengers and predators. Scavengers reuse members of an organization once the organization has broken up. Thus, the presence of scavengers has no effect on the longevity of the organization. On the other hand, a predator can actively hasten the breakup of an organization. Thus, the presence of predators reduces the lifespan of organizations. Once the organization is dead the subsequent actions of scavengers and predators are almost exactly the same.

When organizational death happens, re-users at all levels get to feast. If they are early enough, the re-users may be able to pull out wholly functioning subgroups of entities, i.e. "organs" which have a specific role and function but are incapable of independent existence. If this does not work, then perhaps individual entities can be recovered. If that too does not work, then perhaps the sub-entities can be salvaged.

As an example, when an animal dies, its organs can be re-used, or its cells, or its protein, lipid and carbohydrate molecules. The higher the level of reuse, the less the effort to build up sub-organizations again. Sometimes the reuse goes back only one layer, i.e. the entities are used as they are. For example, some sea slugs (cnidosacs) directly reuse the stinger cells of their prey in their own defense. Sometimes the reuse reverts back down more than one layer. When an animal digests food it does not use the cells of the prey, but breaks it down one more layer into macro-molecules. Mergers and acquisitions are a regular feature of human corporations, although from most of the outcomes one can argue that the consuming organizations often get severe indigestion.

There can be two types of predators. The first are those who are also organizations composed of similar members. We shall call this horizontal predation. An example of this is tigers and deer, both of which are composed of very similar cells. The size of the predator can be quite different from that of the prey. Zebra eat grass and are much larger than it is. On the other hand, malaria parasites are much smaller than both the humans and the mosquitoes they infect, even though they too are multi-cellular. Horizontal predators and their prey exist at the same level of organization, but form different species.

The second kind of predators are those who are at a different level, often the lower level. We shall call this vertical predation. An example of these would be bacterial infections of animals, since bacteria are single cells, while the animal is a multi-cellular organization. For viral infections, the difference is two levels, since viruses are essentially large molecules. Vertical predators and their "prey" exist at different levels of organization.

A valid conjecture is that the bacterium is not really interested in consuming the whole animal. Instead it is interested in one particular cell. That cell just happens to be a part of the animal. Similarly, the virus does not really care about the cell. Instead it is interested in specific molecules which just happen to be part of the cell.

Some organizations are always tempted to steal parts of similar organizations and reuse them. Directly raiding almost identical organizations (i.e. widely practiced cannibalism) would normally be evolutionary suicide.

7.4   Symbiotes

For symbiotic relationships it is instructive to hypothesize on possible origin narratives. Many symbiotic relationships are same-level, for example both butterflies and plants are multi-cellular organizations. However, the symbiosis did not occur as soon as plants and insects came into being (plants came first, one sup-poses).

Both pollinating insects and flowers originated on land about 125 million years ago. Before that plants and insects evolved as predators and prey. Some examples of plants and their pollinat-ing insects are so closely intertwined (and strange) that they are clearly the result of many steps taken together down a common path.

On the other hand, many symbiotic relationships are asym-metrical. For example, consider the relationship between multi-cellular animals and their gut bacteria (as well as other bacteria on their body). This has multi-cellular organisms on one side, and single-celled organisms on the other. We can hypothesize that if indeed all multi-cellular animal have gut bacteria, then this co-existence may have started even before multi-cellular animals came about.

Perhaps in a colony some bacteria were better than others in metabolizing a specific food source. Over time co-evolution may have resulted in the construction of this symbiosis- the gut bacteria focused on their core competence, and the animal was responsible for (literally) feeding this population. This may have initially been a predatory relationship, since the inefficient cells would have had to consume the more efficient cells to steal their bio-matter. Cows and other herbivores continue to have large populations of gut bacteria, and it is these bacteria which digest the food that the cow eats. The cow then digests the bacteria in another part of their compound stomach.

In some cases the symbiosis may occur halfway between levels. All animal cells have structures called mitochondria which help translate food into energy for the cell's use. These are actually cells within cells, and have their own DNA from a time when cells perhaps had not yet collected all DNA into their nucleus. Mitochondrial DNA serves as an independent historical record, and is passed from mother to daughter (it is also passed from mother to son, but has conventionally been lost since the egg gets only the mother's mitochondria). Perhaps there was a time when some cells were just better than others in converting food into energy.

A similar example is that of chloroplasts in both multi-cellular and single-celled plants. These symbiotic relationships are often so strong that we have to search very hard to find examples where only one exists without the other. But they do exist. Perhaps there is an organizational overhead from keeping mitochondria or chloroplasts that pays off only above a certain size, or only in certain conditions.

7.5   Evolutionary Consequences of Re-users

Predators drive organization (prey) evolution. This, in turn, drives predator evolution as well. Scavenger evolution, on the other hand, is not co-evolutionary.

Horizontal predators help the prey population (not the prey, but prey populations) in different ways. Predators cull the weak from the prey population, thus pushing the prey along one dimension of evolution. This comes back to hurt individual predators by making it more difficult to hunt prey, and hence pushes the predator population in the same dimension of evolution. If for some reason the prey population vanishes, the predator population may also perish, unless it has multiple potential target species. On the other hand, if the predator cannot keep up with the evolving prey, then the pressure to evolve is lesser. Thus, predator and prey attributes evolve into an equilibrium depending upon functional efficiency factors like metabolism.

Some vertical predators drive prey to figure out other defenses. Plants develop many alkaloids, including nicotine and cannabinoids, in order to deter insects and animals from eating them. While some bacteria may prefer a specific host, many "harmful" bacteria can jump species, for example from one primate to another, or from cows to humans, or across different species of birds. Thus, they are not as tied to one species for their survival (as a species). This is probably because all those different hosts use similar functional entities for necessary tasks. Thus, a bacteria which has a preference for skin cells is almost equally at home on the skin cells of many different animals.

Thus, a vertical predator's prey may not be able to evolve a better defense mechanism since that resides at a lower organizational level than the one the prey is active in.

For example, our cells may not be able to suddenly synthesize antibiotics, and may not be able to incorporate the learning from various fungi which can synthesize antibiotics, since we no longer share biological exchange mechanisms with them. Similarly, while some single cells may be able to evolve against viruses and bacteriophages by changing their surface chemistry, those evolutionary pathways may be currently unavailable to large animals.

7.6   Organizational Robustness

Consider the predator-prey relationship from the point of view of the organizations composed of each. The relationship between the herd of predators and the herd of prey may be considered symbiotic since it (mostly) eliminates weaker entities in both herds and helps both herds become better in a functional dimension[1].

The risks to the prey from horizontal predation can evolve into symbiosis. But in the case of vertical predation this is more difficult. For example, a virus may attack a cell, but if that cell is really important, the death of the cell due to the virus can cause the death of the multi-cellular organization of which the cell was a part. The organization evolves at a slower pace than the attacking entity and may always be at a disadvantage.

Thus organizations must build robustness through redundancy and overlap. If possible, they must ensure that the removal of a single entity does not jeopardize the organization, and they must also ensure that they have a surplus to spare to nurture symbiotic partnerships.

---

[1]Going in the other direction, and with a different example, the symbiotic relationships between trees and creeper vines looks rather more predatory when viewed from the point of view of the cells of the tree and the vine.

Chapter 8

Life and Death

Many generations of innocent youngsters have lamented the presence of death in the world. Many imaginative artists have written fantasies exploring the consequences of an actual physical immortal among us. Yet death exists, and will continue to exist in all layers as long as the world exists. In this chapter we will explore the role of death for organizations across all levels.

Some of the questions you can ask for yourself are

- What is the "normal" lifetime of entities? What is the "normal" lifetime of the organizations of entities?

- What are some examples of "premature" demise of organizations?

- How are the strategies of successful organizations replicated? What happens to the less successful organizations?

The concept of death and its relation to the other concepts is shown in Figure 8.1. Death is a critical part of evolution.

An organization's lifespan is not tied to the lifespan of its entities. Proto-organizations may survive much shorter time spans than the component entities, but stable organizations usually have longer lifespans than their entities. Thus, there are many entities that spend their entire lives as part of the same organization. Yet, sooner or later, the organization must die.

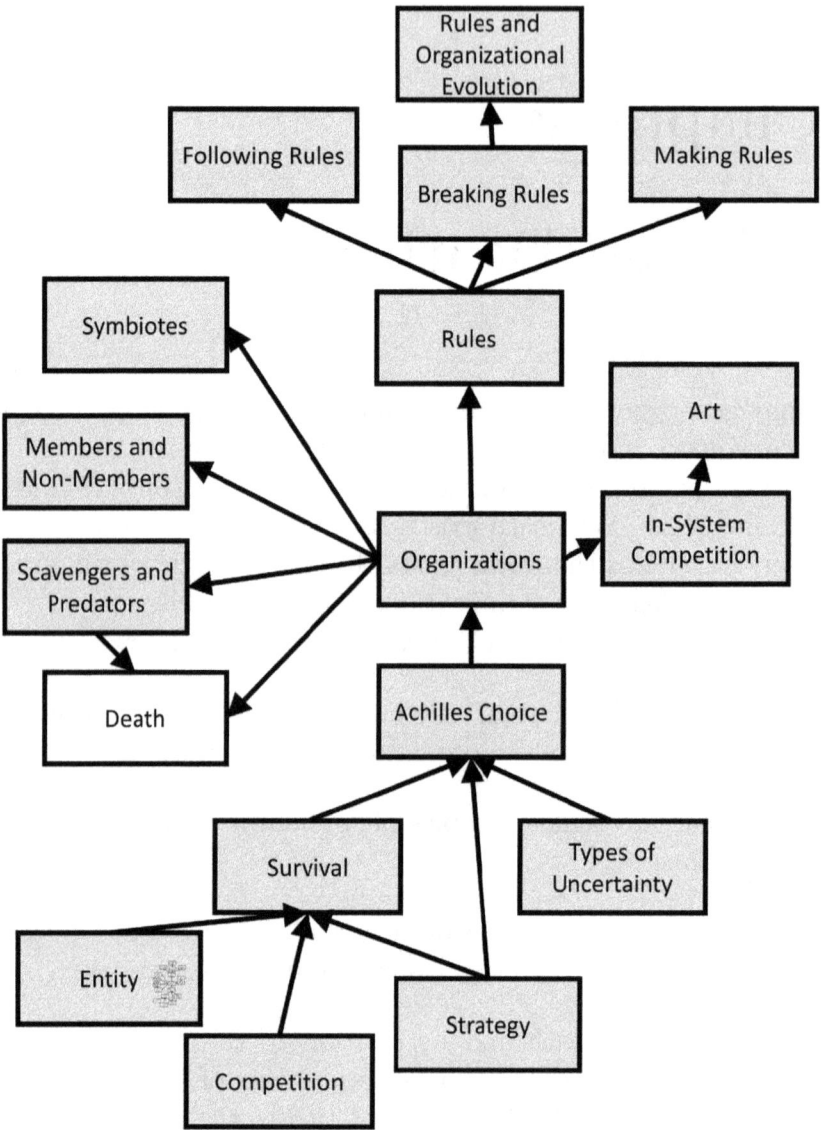

Figure 8.1: Chapter 8 Map: Death

Must an organization die? Maybe not. If an organization can figure out how to compete using its very slow-evolving genetic code then it may be able to live forever, which is just another way of saying that an organization cannot live forever.

8.1 Death

Death occurs when the organization ceases to function.

It may happen due to starvation, when the organizational niche simply dries up (sometimes literally like a puddle).

On the other hand, it may happen due to external causes and natural accidents. This can be called untimely death. For example, out-of-system competition may result in death from legal, biological, physical, chemical or other attacks.

Finally, internal causes can also cause an untimely death. Before the organization stabilizes, entities can "disagree" and disperse, causing the organization's death. We can also have too few entities "working" to support the entire organization, causing its collapse.

Some types of death are termed "timely", i.e. from "old age". The exact definition of old age changes with the context. As has happened over the past couple of centuries for humans, lifespans can increase dramatically due to medicine and hygiene. Sometimes timely death occurs when the deterioration of organizational defenses allows asymmetric (smaller) predators to overwhelm the organization (e.g. a bacterial infection for humans). Sometimes timely death occurs due to the physical breakdown of some vital mechanism, which would lead to a decay of the organization even in the absence of smaller predators (e.g., a heart attack).

The "normal" lifetime of any member is the outcome of the interplay of many opposing forces. What a member gains from one genetic advantage is balanced out by a disadvantage in another dimension. There is no single optimal "normal" lifespan of a species. Among mammals there are those that live for a few months, and those that can live to almost a century. There are small creatures who are extremely vulnerable to death from predators, while there are others so large that they have no effective predators. There are creatures who can regenerate a large body part, who still live very short lives. Many "normal" lifetime strategic choices play out among us simultaneously, and we have no way of determining one as better than the other.

After the death of an animal we expect that the cells that had full membership of the animal will also die. On the other hand, some of the gut and skin bacterial may survive because they were symbiotes and may be able to transfer to other animals.

Similarly, upon the death of a cell, molecules which are integral to the cell will break down, e.g., its DNA or other proteins. Intermediate molecules like proteins may break down, or they may be consumed/used by other cells. Simple molecules like water will not change at all.

On the dissolution of a business firm we expect that it is the "company men" who will find it most difficult to find employment afterwards. These are the employees who identified the deepest with the firm, whose position in it depended upon a deep knowledge of the firm and whose careers had gained the most from a long association with the firm.

8.2 The Necessity of Death

One of the Utopian concepts of some naive writers involves the banishment of death. For human-scale stories, this may involve living "thousands" of years. Ignoring the fact that a being living thousands (or even millions) of years is still mortal, this will not work, competitively speaking.

If "suddenly" a member was able to live significantly longer than its peers (and this change helped it live better, for example, by being able to use its knowledge for a longer period of time), then this survival advantage would quickly spread across the population in a few generations[1]. Thus, relative longevity is

---

[1]This is an example of how even small advantages that enable a member of a species find more mates, more food, or have more offspring can gradually build up over generations by causing each successive generation to have a

a transient incident. This would quickly reach equilibrium across the member population. This does not take away from the pain of those members who were denied this advantage, and must either themselves die, or see their descendants lose out. This has happened countless times across the entire span of life and evolution on earth.

An entity is a representation of a certain strategy, as we have mentioned. This strategy may be written down in its chemistry, or its genetic code, or its standard operating manuals.

However, an entity is also an amalgamation of entities at the earlier (or lower) level. A human is an amalgamation of cells. Thus, each of the lower-level entities is also a representation of a certain strategy. Carry this back to the lower levels, and it is clear that a given entity is a representation of a particular strategy at every level of organization at its own level and below.

At the same time, there are free entities at every other level. Humans exist in the same environment where there are bacteria, viruses and unaffiliated chemical compounds. Each of the entities at the different levels is the manifestation of a particular strategy to deal with survival in the specific physical, chemical, biological and organizational environment it finds itself in.

As the environment changes the specific strategy represented in the entity becomes less and less appropriate. Competitive forces will continue to drive the evolution of all entities at all lower levels. But the organization itself prevents the evolution of entities in it at a particular level. Thus, a cell in a human body continues with most of its genetic code from the birth of the human, while the bacteria and viruses around it continue to evolve and try to find a way to break down its defenses. Even with clever methods of protection (like a learning immune system), there is an increasing gap between the abilities of the entities in an organization and the entities in the environment around it.

Death itself is an equilibrium between the costs of maintaining an outdated organization and the benefits of the organization.

---

larger fraction of the progeny of the originally advantaged individual. This assumes, of course, that the specific advantage transmits, can be learned, or can be inherited from parent to offspring.

There is nothing natural about a "natural" lifespan. It can and does change with new technology. Even with such changes the lifespan of an organization is finite.

8.3   The Importance of Death

On a personal level, death is one of the most disruptive concepts for an individual to comprehend. For members who have never known life outside the system, and have grown up in a benign environment, death often requires a radical rethinking of their own understanding of how the world works. Yet death is omnipresent, at every level.

Any system tries to handle the consequences of death in order to achieve two opposing objectives at the same time. First, it tries to ensure continuity in the face of member death. Second, it tries to use death as a means to ensure membership and compliance.

Any member's death usually causes disruption to the system proportionate to the member's role in the organization. Sometimes the disruption may be disproportionate if random factors are aligned in a manner that causes the disruption to cascade through the other parts of the system. Thus, unless a system plans for some degree of redundancy, it will be at the mercy of the inevitable deaths of its members. While this is a necessary risk when the organization is small, beyond a certain size the organization may plan some redundancy. This is another overhead that the organization must cover, as mentioned earlier in Section 7.6[2].

Ironically, while the threat of death drives members into an organization, it does not eliminate death. Thus, the organization must come up with a mechanism to handle the impact of the death of a member on the membership intent of all other members.

Organizations also use a death to remind members that if the

---

[2]In extreme cases, an organization can use planned redundancy where any specific member is responsible for a task for a fixed period of time and is replaced by the next member. For example, skin and blood cells live for only a few months.

organization were not there, this event would be more frequent and more traumatic to them. A career-ending injury in a sports league reminds players that but for the rules maintained by the league such injuries would be far more common.

Chapter 9

Conclusion

In summary, the framework presented in the preceding chapters in this part establishes that the tendency of some entities in a layer to survive lead to systems which allow them to survive longer. This happens even when these are not conscious or thinking entities. This process gives rise to organizations, which are systems that provide a promise of longer existence for the entities that are part of it when compared with unaffiliated entities. This process may not immediately give rise to organizations, and it may be disrupted many times if changing conditions create more efficient entities or organizations. Finally, as soon as an efficient organization is established, within in a small number of lifetimes, many (perhaps most) of the entities also organize into similar organizations. At this point it is appropriate to change our mental orientation and think of these similar organizations as the entities in the next level.

For an example, in the early stages of our solar system, when the earth cooled down, it allowed many types of atoms to coalesce into stable molecules. As conditions changed further, it allowed these molecules to self-organize into proto-cells, which then took a really long time to make the next step to multi-cellular beings, both plant and animals.

For another example, as the tools of human industry and communication changed, we evolved from nomadic families into tribes living in villages, to nationalities living in cities. As these tools continue to evolve within our lifetimes, we see tremendous stress and change in the human institutions of businesses, religions and nations.

We have opened each chapter in this part by asking you to answer some questions about the entities and organizations that you are interested in. Perhaps you are a biologist who studies cells, or insects, or chimpanzees. Perhaps you are a sociologist looking at remote isolated tribes, or the digital natives of early twenty-first century. Perhaps you are a physicist who models quarks and atoms. For each of you this framework leaves many unanswered questions, and we hope you will provide us with both the questions and the answers.

In this final chapter of this part, we will step back and consider some broad differences across the layers we laid out at the beginning, in Chapter 2. As we said, the framework applies itself most naturally to a small range of layers, perhaps from macro-molecules to social organizations. Even within them, though, there are significant and crucial differences.

9.1 Differences Across Layers

There are many aspects that change dramatically across layers. The nature of competition, the rules that entities follow, and the nature and impact of organizations of those entities. Some of this is shown in Table 9.1. Since we are not certain of the answers, many of these differences will have to remain as unanswered questions for now.

9.1.1 Competition

If sub-atomic particles "compete", what do they compete for? Do molecules compete for atoms?

In addition to these questions, it is also clear that two molecules competing for atoms "in the wild" is quite different from two molecules in a cell competing for atoms. We may even use analogous terms like "cooperation" and "well-behaved" when document-

	Evolution	Rule Type	Creates Rules
Subatomic	Frozen	Nuclear	No
Molecules	Environmental	Molecular	No
Cells	Generations	DNA	No?
Multi-cellular	Generations	DNA, Neural	Sometimes
Social/Firms	"Faster"	Social, Legal	Yes
Economies	"Faster"	?	Yes

Table 9.1: Behavior across Layers

ing the behavior of molecules in a cell. Yet this continues only as long as the cell is alive. The self-regulatory nature of cells actually channels the competitive nature of molecules through the process of surrounding it with a particular set of other molecules that moderate its behavior.

Similarly, two scientists working in the same research lab compete intensely, but a successful and prominent lab surrounds them with a certain culture (which can be defined as the shared past interactions and behavior and future expectations of behavior of every person in the organization) that channels this raw competitive nature and makes the lab more successful than merely the sum of its parts.

9.1.2 Evolution

The nature of evolution is also different in each layer.

It is not clear when the evolution of subatomic forces may have happened, if indeed it ever did. There is a lot of evidence from conjectural physics about the first few moments after the hypothesized big bang, when the fundamental nature of our universe was determined. Perhaps as we discover more about those hypothesized moments we will learn more about how neutrons and protons came to be. Perhaps there are parallel universes which are organizational dead ends, where there has been and always will be a soup of subatomic particles which cannot decide how to organize since some aspect of their universe is just a little (or a lot) off.

Under normal earth conditions subatomic particles do not usually compete and evolve. They are probably in a state of dynamic equilibrium, which allows us to ignore them since they appear stable to other layers above them. Conditions inside the sun are conjectured to be different, and this is a good thing, for all life on earth depends on this evolutionary fight between subatomic particles (also known as nuclear fusion). Compared to the nature of evolution in higher layers, the activity in the subatomic layer can usually be summarized very nicely by simpler equations described by physicists (the equations themselves are evolving, due to intense competition between physicists, but that is another story). Even this is a simplification- occasionally there are conditions on earth that allow for subatomic rearrangements- nuclear explosions.

From the atomic and molecular stage onward we have a better idea of how evolution works, mainly because we can run experiments and see how these are organized. All around us these phenomena continue to create and break down matter. But the rules are set, probably from the initial moment of creation. A sodium atom and a chlorine atom will always want to dance together when they meet. These are more in the domain of permanent rules of physics, rather than issues that each atom gets to decide for itself each time it sees another atom. Molecules are present in a large range of environmental conditions under which they evolve. We see new molecules and new types of molecules being created in the soil, in the sea, in deep sea thermal vents, and many other niche environments. On the other hand, inside living cells the evolution of molecules proceeds along very well-defined paths determined by billions of generations of cells which have themselves evolved on the basis of these molecular evolutionary paths.

As we go up the layers, the basics of the evolutionary processes stay the same, but the forms are still new and wondrous. Bacteria continue to evolve in response to the various changes in their environments caused by layers far higher than them. Higher concentrations of certain metals previously known only in trace amounts (like copper and arsenic from human activities like mining) force them to try internal molecular pathways that account for these higher concentrations (on a related note, multi-cellular organisms respond much slower to these metals since they live longer and have to follow the same genetic template, and thus suffer from heavy metal poisoning). Higher concentrations of plant molecules that were previously encountered only in certain rare plants are now seen by larger number of bacteria, and hence must also be countered by them, giving rise to multi-resistant strains of bacteria which give nightmares to human doctors and epidemiologists.

For both single-cells and animals, evolution is inter-generational, which means that a given entity is stuck with the genes they were gifted at birth, subject to small changes driven by their immune systems. This also means that evolution is a death-driven process, from the demise of those individual single-cells and animals who are slightly more susceptible to the change or attack that is underway. Finally, for social organizations or firms, and countries and economies, evolution may occur even between generations, as a particular entity morphs into a completely different form. (Perhaps that may be due to the possibility that they are not completely "formed", and that a lot of transfer of entities is possible across their boundaries.)

9.1.3   Information Processing Capabilities

The fundamental difference when we get to organizations created from more information-capable entities like mammals and specifically humans is the speed of evolution.

Pre-information organizations evolve across generations. Thus, for example the changes from mother cell to daughter cell are rather minimal when they reproduce by division (asexually), and the only changes are random mutations. The changes in cells with sexual reproduction is a bit more dramatic, but the nature of species puts constraints on how radical these changes can be. It is often more of a variation across a spectrum of parameter values (for example, how much of a particular protein the cell tends to produce).

This basic template does not change during the lifetime of the organization, mostly. Cells have the ability to keep dormant banks of DNA and switch them on or off based on environmental triggers. They may also have the ability to incorporate strands of DNA from other creatures they come in contact with, thus increasing the store of DNA knowledge for later use.

Information organizations seem to be a completely different phenomena. In case of human organizations, they evolve within a generation. The organization changes from month to month, or from year to year. This is a timescale that is shorter than not only the organization's lifetime, but also much shorter than the component entity lifetimes (i.e. human lifetimes). For many human organizations, like businesses, religions, nations and economic systems, this evolution is intra-generational. The system adapts to different conditions without dying. Perhaps this is due to the fact that these systems are not that cohesive. There is a constant flow of entities in and out of these organizations. This allows for a change in internal processes, systems and skills that is usually not possible in, say, a cell, which regulates its boundary far more fiercely. Perhaps this too shall morph into inter-generational change if we have super-cohesive organizations, e.g. a clan of clones whose allegiance is to their group identity (for example similar molecular DNA or similar belief systems).

Is this the nature of this layer (and subsequent layers)? Or is this a temporary phase in the formation of organizations in the face of blinding fast advances in communication and information technologies? If it is the latter, we may indeed conjecture that at some time in the future (perhaps hundreds of years later), we will see organizations that use every possible communication technology in an integrated manner so that individual humans are as much a part of the organization as individual cells are in our own bodies. It is possible then that individual human lifetimes may be as short compared to the organizational lifetime as our cells' few months are compared to our own lives. Perhaps this is the nature of evolution in layers above multi-cellular beings, and we shall always observe intra-generational change in them.

9.1.4 Rule Type and Rule Creation

As a final category of difference, consider the nature of rules in entities. (There are many other categories of differences across layers which we must collectively address in the future).

What are the rules of behavior and competition, when did they first get codified, and finally, do they change at all?

At one level it seems that for subatomic, atomic and molecular layers, the rules are actively described by the sciences of physics and chemistry (including quantum physics and bio-chemistry). While we have mapped out these laws for only a small set of conditions, we have an almost blind faith in our ability to uncover the rules of behavior for the entities in these layers given enough time and experimental resources. For example, it is only a matter of time (albeit centuries or millennia) before we will be able to understand the chemistry of the upper cloud layers in Jupiter and either discover or invent a biochemistry based on that context. As many speculative fiction writers have written, one day we may even be able to design creatures which look like humans, but whose underlying biochemistry is designed to operate in completely different conditions.

However, in the layers after multi-cellular animals, there seems to be no consensus on what the rules of engagement and organization creation should be. There are rules based on religious proclamations, and organizations of humans known as religions, spanning different geographies, languages and cuisines. There are rules based (originally) on geographic location/origin, which are called countries. There are other sets of rules which give rise to business organizations, artistic groups, and many other attributes.

Each of these classes of organizations uses a bewildering variety of rules, and many classes frequently change the rules in order to adapt to changing circumstances, or even changing attributes of their members. They freely split, merge or re-emerge in radically different forms. Consider the changes in the Christian religion over the 20th century and beyond, or the changes in the nature of the Chinese economy from 1980 to 2010 and later.

It is a matter of conjecture whether early molecular mecha-

nisms which supported cellular life were similarly fluid in the first
billion years of life on earth. It is quite possible that what we
see as a single comprehensive theory of biochemistry of all living
cells is actually the result of many millions of years of intense
evolution resulting from the competition between different molecular pathways, perhaps separated by a thin margin of efficiency
or marginally better integration with other pathways.

If that is the nature of evolution, then we are a long way away.
Different companies order supplies in wildly different ways, and
pay their suppliers on many disparate and mutually contradictory
business processes and information technology systems. On the
other hand, some firms are able to build quite stable ecosystems
(in the context of hardware and software change), which may be
the basis for the next level of organization. Some businesses are
gradually moving towards comprehensive social-media-like mobile
platforms that they expect their employees to use all the time.
Some countries are also moving towards similar all-encompassing
payment and social safety net systems that will leave little variation in a certain set of activities. Whether any of these systems
provides a competitive advantage over the others may also be difficult to predict.

9.2 Final Conjectures

9.2.1 Above and Below

One conjecture is whether the framework can be extended "lower".
Thus, are nuclear particles the organizational form of various sub-
entities? Today we may not know enough of quantum physics to
be able to definitively answer this question.

On the other end of the spectrum, can humans be fully aware
of any such organizations that may or may not exist above the
level of the organizations that we participate in? Can a molecule
be aware of the dog it belongs to, even if it is vaguely "aware" of
the cell it is a member of?

9.2.2 Natural Forces and Information Density

There is another interplay that is quite interesting across all these layers. This is the importance of natural forces compared to information.

The forces keeping entities together are weaker at the higher levels of organization. At the subatomic level the forces that are at play are extremely powerful. Nuclear forces are powerful, but the forces that lie in the quantum level are probably a few orders of magnitude more powerful than nuclear forces. When atoms form molecules there are mildly strong forces that bind atoms together. However, when molecules become large and create cells, the forces are much weaker in nature. The attachment between cells depends upon the weakest of molecular forces, and in some cases these can be overpowered quite easily. Finally, in social groups formed by various animals we have a lot of digging to uncover whether there are any forces in play at all.

In social groups of multi-cellular organisms the signaling between these organisms forms the basis of the social group. As we go from one layer to another the strength of "natural" forces decreases, and the importance of signaling and information processing increases (along with the increased ability of the entities to send, receive and process such information).

Even within a layer we have different species of entities that create organizations of different complexity based on their ability to process information. For example, bee hives and human tribes, both of which are composed of multi-cellular entities, have different levels of information density. Even among human organizations there are simple social organizations, and globe-spanning multi-national organizations that use a wide variety of communication and information processing technologies.

9.2.3 The Nature of Evolution

This brings us to a very fundamental difference between the layers-the nature of evolution. While evolution itself is different in each layer, it seems to us (at least in this universe) that there is much more stability in the process of evolution in the earlier layers. However, as we organize up to, say, groups of multi-cellular organisms, evolution itself becomes context specific.

Perhaps we can look back and see a time when multi-cellular organizations had not yet stabilized, and such organizations formed, evolved and broke up at a pace much faster than the individual cells' lifetimes. We probably have no evidence of how long this lasted, other than the evolutionary record showing the time span between the emergence of single-celled creatures and multi-cellular beings.

(Remainder of the page is blank)

(Blank page)

9.2.4   About Other Layer Frameworks

There are a few other areas where there are layers. One prominent area is in the conceptual organization of computer-based processing, and in the related area of digital communications. Let us explore how the concepts presented so far apply to these areas.

Computers are conceptualized as layers. At the risk of over-simplifying, we can begin with the basic layer where everything is represented as 0s and 1s (each such 0 or 1 is called a bit), i.e. the binary layer. These are organized into groups of a fixed length, collecting 8 or multiples of 8 into bytes or words or similar definitions. These are then conceptualized on the processing side as specific instructions for the processor to complete a task. These build up to processing threads, programs, and enterprise systems.

Digital communications as well as digital data are similar- they start from bits, which are organized into digital words, each of which may represent an English or Chinese letter, which are themselves organized into words, and so on.

For our framework, however, these are not independent entities competing against each other in each layer. A specific computer bit does not compete with another bit and then decide to form a computer word with 15 other bits in order to improve their chances of survival. Thus, our competitive framework does not directly apply to computer processing, data and communication layers.

On the other hand, there are companies, industry associations, independent standards groups and non-profits that operate in the industries focused on each of these layers who are actually competing rather intensely. Thus, these technology standards are the tools of competition for these companies. These standards and protocols live or die based on the business success of these business entities. From that perspective, our framework applies to these industries quite well.

The End

That brings us to the end of the conjectures that we hope provide a brief view of where this framework may be applied. As an analogy, physics does not say "In large quantities over long times, the hydrogen atom can give rise to galaxies, stars, metals, planets and even life." Similarly, this framework does not claim to predict what evolving organizations and layers can look like. There is far too much complexity in their interactions, and far too many possibilities for us to map out in a predictive manner.

At best it may help our understanding of some of the tasks we go through in our daily lives as we carry on, mostly oblivious to the workings of the larger organizations in which we are explicitly and implicitly embedded.

Part II

Parables and Commandments

Chapter 10

Preface to Parables and Commandments

We will begin with the applications of the concepts that are laid out in a more structured way in Part I. These applications are divided into two main categories.

(For convenience, it may help to provide brief definitions of three terms: layers, entities, and organizations. Layers are levels of organization into which we can divide the world around us. These can be atoms, molecules, cells, multi-cellular creatures, organizations, nations and so on. Entities are similar beings which inhabit a layer. Finally, organizations are collections of entities in one layer which help define entities in the next layer of the universe. Thus, molecules are organizations of atoms, and nations are organizations of humans. The main framework proposes a process by which entities may come together and create organizations.)

This section begins with a collection of incidents and observations from the universe around us, with explanations that follow from the concepts in Part I. Thus, we start with some parables of layers and organizations. These are interesting stories which are selected for their applicability to other layers, or for their demonstration of the interactions across layers.

Following this, we come up with a small number of commandments for entities in four representative positions with respect to organizations. This is important because interactions between entities is the force that gives rise to the next layer of organization under the right conditions. These four representative entities are (a) the complete believer inside the organization, (b) the prince or leader at the top of the organization, (c) the symbiote living in the shadows of the organization and (d) the entity living far away from any organization. These commandments are not exhaustive. Many more can be written and the few written here can be refined for specific circumstances. Similarly, the four representative positions are by no means exhaustive. There are many more shades of membership, niche positions and specialty roles that are there in organizations. Each one of these can have a set of representative commandments[1].

We hope that providing instances and applications of the framework may provide the necessary motivation to understand the structured arguments, which are more abstract.

---

[1]As an example, consider the role of police within an organization. A common set of commandments can be written that would apply equally well to policemen in a city, white blood cells in the body, and internal auditors in a corporation. This is the level of abstraction we will try to achieve- it allows for a greater range of application of these concepts, at the cost of not being fully applicable to a specific situation.

Chapter 11

Parables of Organization

Parables

The basic frameworks presented in Part I have been understood for millennia. If we stretch the definition of "understood," then perhaps these words have been understood for as long as there have been social beings. Without stretching definitions too far, the historical evidence for this is all around us. Every religion has a set of commandments. Every nation has a code of conduct, explicit or implicit. Every organization has a set of rules.

What has changed in recent decades is our understanding of entities and objects at the very small and the very large scales of time and space. A philosopher contemplating these things a thousand years ago may not have known the details of layers which are very small, namely the atom or the molecule, or have completely understood the sociological nature of large groups of humans (although to be fair, very large organizations of humans did not exist then in the same tightly knit sense that, say, a modern country, or multi-national firm operates today). However, within the limited few layers that she could see, these principles were very much in play, and could be observed and commented upon.

In addition to our physical and material understanding of objects that have existed for millennia, the technological advances in transportation and communication have themselves enabled the creation of virtual groups that are larger than was possible, say, a thousand years ago. On the communication side, these technologies must include, at the very start, speech and writing all the way to today's machine learning advances. On the transportation side, these include everything from domesticated animals like the bull and the horse, machines like the wheel and the automobile, to aerospace.

The practical distillation of this knowledge, observation and insight has always been used to help create organizations that are more cohesive, and operate "better" than those that existed earlier (i.e. offer these organizations built on "new" principles a survival advantage). This operational knowledge complements the core guiding principles that allow the creation of the organization.

One of the longest surviving group of organizations of humans are religions. Every religion has a core message distilled into principles to live by. These commandments and word-of-God edicts are the longest-lived examples of successful rules used to build social groups.

There are other examples of more nuanced awareness of this framework, often directed at the ruling class of the day. These include Machiavelli's "The Prince", and the collection of words from Chanakya's "Artha Shashtra". It should also be trivial to find similar words archived from any civilization that has lasted more than a few hundred years.

The following examples are grouped into the areas of knowledge from which they are drawn, which are often related to the layer (or layers) across which they apply. As an interesting exercise we can also take each example and explore whether there are similar examples in the other layers.

11.1 Bio-molecules

11.1.1 Human Pandemics in Modern Times

There are numerous microscopic entities which invade humans and other multi-cellular organisms. In the pre-industrial past the scope of many epidemics and pandemics were limited by the very rudimentary communication and transportation channels through which individual people and communities interacted with each other. However, in modern times societies and economies interact much more with each other, through trade and cheap transportation. Thus, these microscopic entities- bacteria, viruses and others- can now affect not just humans, but also economies.

The mad cow disease is caused by a prion, which is smaller than a virus. It is an information disease, which means that it is able to exploit the vulnerability in a cell's genetic code to create additional copies of itself. Back before life as we know it, early ancestors of prions were the first replicating complex molecules. As life became more complex, the basic prion replication has stayed essentially unchanged. This is why mad cow disease emerges spontaneously in a few cows per million.

If prions attack any cell, they kill it in the process of replicating. If prions attack a brain cell, they also compromise the critical processing ability of the animal. If enough brain cells are killed, the animal also dies.

A few years ago the process of recycling unmarketable animal parts by feeding them back to the animals allowed prions to replicate far more abundantly. Thus, it compromised the herd. Since the practice was common all across the US, this affected the entire sector when some countries insisted on banning the import of US beef.

Thus, a complex molecule compromised some cells, which compromised a whole animal, which compromised many herds, which compromised many trading firms, and finally, hurt an economy.

11.1.2 Frozen Competition: A Biochemical Snapshot

Deep inside our bodies there is evidence of an unfinished competition that occurred a long time ago in the biochemistry layer.

Each of us shares the basic genetic template of life with almost every other living being on earth. This is a bio-molecule called DNA, which is a code that can be represented with 4 letters- A,

G, T and C. The human genetic code has about 3 billion letters organized into 23 pairs of chromosomes.

These letters are used to make proteins, which is a critical part of all the biochemical reactions in every cell and body, e.g. digestion, vision, muscle contractions, nerve signals and so on. Proteins are composed of amino acids.

There is an intermediate process step in the codification of DNA to proteins. DNA is organized into groups of 3 letters, for example, AAG, TAC or CCG. Since there are 3 letters and each letter is chosen from an alphabet of 4 letters, there are 64 possible words. However, these words are used to define only 21 amino acids. Thus, different DNA words may represent the same amino acid. This is similar to the redundancy in words in a language, for example house, dwelling and residence mean the same.

Almost all living beings use the same DNA dictionary to define amino acids. In very rare cases there are single-celled organisms that use a different dictionary. Critically, mitochondria, which are the parts of our cells that help in energy conversion, also use a different dictionary. To recap some hypotheses, mitochondria are thought to have been independent cells a long time ago. They were more efficient in energy metabolism and evolved into symbiotic co-existence with all cells.

Thus, our conjecture is that at some point of time early in the evolution of life, there may have been many biochemical dictionaries. At some point of time one of these became associated with an evolutionary advantage and expanded in the population to crowd out all other dictionaries almost everywhere. Perhaps this was directly related to the inherent advantages from the dictionary itself, e.g. a more efficient way of making amino acids. Perhaps there were many almost equally efficient dictionaries, but one of them stumbled upon an unrelated winning advantage. Perhaps it was because an entity using one dictionary figured out how to cooperate with the precursors of mitochondria by offering it protection in return for efficiency in energy conversion.

This is quite similar to the symbiosis between plant cells and chloroplasts; however chloroplasts use the same dictionary as plant and animal cells.

11.1.3　DNA and DNA

The basic genetic code of all living beings is written in their DNA. In tandem with the entity's environment DNA helps determine the specific possibility that comes to fruition from all the options available to the entity at conception.

However, DNA is not very neatly separable. There is DNA, and there is DNA.

First, in the most complex form of organization, DNA is neatly encapsulated in each cell's nucleus, from where it is read to create proteins, and where is it modified to capture new information. Second, in older forms of cells the DNA resides in the cell, but not in a nucleus- it resides in a soup along with all the other organelles in the cell. In both these cases we call this DNA the cell's identity.

On the other hand, in every cell there are small strands of DNA called plasmids. Plasmids do their own thing, which is the same as what "proper" DNA strands do: serve as templates for protein generation. However, while "central" DNA replicates only when a cell divides into two, plasmids replicate many times in between. Folks have conjectured that the concentration and activity levels of these various plasmids may be behind some diseases and deficiencies.

Then of course, there is a separate lineage of DNA within mitochondria (which help with harnessing chemical energy from sugars) and chloroplasts (which help in photosynthesis in plants).

And finally, there is DNA in large viruses, which gets injected into cells during a viral attack. This DNA harnesses the normal machinery of the cell and subverts it into producing more copies of itself, often killing the cell in this process.

In bacteria and other rough-and-tumble cells there is a vigorous exchange of DNA fragments. This process shares the DNA from many cells without the entire ceremony of reproduction. It is like companies hiring away executives from their competitors in order to get new ideas and strategies.

At a level of abstraction, one could even conjecture that life is all about blind competition between different DNA fragments:

those that reside in viruses, those that are in cells, but are independent, and those that are central to the cell (as well as many variants in between). Other than providing a venue for their activities, cells and super-cellular organizational structures (like elephants, sharks or bees) are rather peripheral side-effects[1].

11.2 Biology

11.2.1 The Flower and the Butterfly

Plants did not always have flowers. In fact, the earliest insects, who evolved after the plants, were quite problematic for plants, since the latter had very few defenses against them. Biochemical defenses that had been used against bacteria and fungi were slow-evolving, and some parts of plants were always susceptible to insect predators.

There are various ways in which plants co-opted these thieves, and the most beautiful (at least to human eyes) are flowers. This must have happened accidentally, with some genetic material transferred from plant to plant through the mouths and feet of insects. After that it was the slow evolution of both of them. Plants developed specialized parts with even more attractive sap (i.e. sweet nectar), as well as signage to visually indicate availability (flower petals). Insects developed specialized mouth parts to probe deep into the flowers to suck out the nectar. As a payoff to the plants, the germ cells in the form of pollen evolved into positions most likely to be picked up by insects and transported to other flowers.

This co-evolution arose from competition and theft, not from benign design. Hidden in this co-evolution are answers to more complex questions of why some insects choose to visit only flowers of one type in a foraging session.

Finally, the question of why humans find both flowers and butterflies "beautiful" and spend lots of effort to nourish and sustain,

---

[1] Also described as "the selfish gene", a la Richard Dawkins. Our knowledge of DNA has progressed a lot since the time the good doctor wrote his book- it is now quite a wild world down there.

is a question we will leave for the future.

11.2.2 The Chloroplast

One of the early disruptors (from a human point of view) in the story of life was the discovery of chlorophyll, which all plants use to trap solar energy into molecules of sugar. It happened early in the tree of life on earth, and was not instantaneously harnessed by all the extant single-celled life forms. Upon the harnessing of chlorophyll these cells no longer had to forage for energy, or to hunt other cells to consume. Over millions of generations these cells became quite efficient at photosynthesis, and lost many of the other abilities. Thus, they themselves became quite desirable as prey.

Some of them may have evolved defenses against the non-photosynthesizing predatory cells. However, at some point of time a few of the photo-synthesizers developed a symbiosis with the predatory cells, Eventually they co-evolved to such a close symbiosis that the photo-synthesizers began to reside completely within the cells of the others. For some reason this was so efficient that all the multi-cellular plants we see have this structure- each plant cell contains within itself a number of "chloroplast" bodies, which is where all the chlorophyll is located.

This again, is a close symbiosis that co-evolved out of competition and predatory behavior. Why is this more efficient? I do not know.

11.2.3 Malaria, Mosquitoes and Humans

Mosquitoes have been sucking the blood of many animals for millions of years. Malaria, of which there are several varieties, is a single-celled organism which may spend a part of its life in mosquitoes, and a part in humans. The transfer of malaria occurs during the mosquito bite (from the mosquito to the human) and the subsequent extraction of blood (from the human to the mosquito).

By itself a mosquito is a minor irritant. However, with the addition of malaria, mosquitoes become far more lethal. Humans have spent quite some time and effort to eradicate mosquitoes, but it is nothing personal. Mosquitoes, on the other hand, have managed to survive and become resistant to many of the chemicals and other agents used by humans. The main objective, is, of course, to eliminate malaria. Much of the difficulty involves rapidly mutating proteins in the malaria cells which can defeat efforts to target those proteins to disrupt the malaria's biochemistry.

Recent tools used by humans against mosquitoes have included physical devices like bed nets, introduction of sterile mosquitoes in the population, and lasers. If efforts to develop a malaria vaccine succeed, then the human pressure to eradicate mosquitoes may also abate.

11.2.4   The Inequality in the Human Body

Let us compare the benefits of being a nerve cell in the human body, against being a red blood cell.

Assume that the adult human lifetime is at least 50 years long. The average human being weighs about 150 pounds, of which the brain weighs about 3 pounds. However, the brain consumes about 40% of the energy and oxygen that the entire body uses. Thus, 2% of the body mass consumes 40% of the body's resources. That itself means that each day a nerve cell takes up 30 times the resources an average non-nerve cell consumes.

The disparity does not end there. The lifetime of a red blood cell is about 3 months, whereas the lifetime of a nerve cell is almost the same as that of the adult human body, i.e. 50 years. This means that the nerve cell lives about 200 times longer.

Combining these two it appears that the average nerve cell is blessed with wealth that is 1,500 times more than that which accrues to a red blood cell, at least in the human body. (On a related note, at any time the human body has "only" 86 billion nerve cells, and about 25 trillion red blood cells, that is, almost 300 times more- that is 15,000 more red blood cells than nerve cells over the human's lifetime).

We can see this disparity play out in every organization. The natural order does not claim that the resources within an organization will be spread equally across all members. In fact all that matters is whether any specific rule on the internal distribution of wealth increases the chances of survival of the organization in competition with other organizations.

Recent studies of business organizations have found that CEOs make about 100 to 200 times the median annual salary of all employees in the organization. Except for a few organizations where the CEO is the original founder, in many cases the tenures of CEOs may actually be smaller than that of the median employee. This means that the disparity over the period of employment is smaller than this multiple.

There is, however, one area which is significantly different. If a multi-cellular organism dies, then both the skin cell and the nerve cell die. On the other hand, if a business organization dies, many employees (CEOs and janitors alike) often find employment in similar roles elsewhere.

11.2.5   Policing and Auto-Immune Conditions

Every organization beyond a certain size needs an internal police to take on the specialized duty of internal enforcement of member rules. This gives rise to a certain tension between the proportion and efficiency of police and rule breakers.

We have stated earlier that when a norm crystallizes into a rule, it immediately defines rule breakers. A norm allows for a wide range of behavior which is moderated only by peer disapproval. On the other hand, a rule is a line in the sand which should never be crossed. However, if no member ever breaks the rules, then the police are an unnecessary drag on the organization. On the other hand, if there are no police to enforce rules then the rule itself loses teeth, which causes rule breakers to proliferate. The dynamics of police and rule breakers over time is similar to predator-prey population dynamics. It is different mainly in that there is another control cycle in every organization which can ramp up police production if the number of rule breakers exceeds a certain threshold.

Some folks wish for a world where there is no war. Some wish for a world with no rule breakers. Sometimes, the environment conspires to almost make that happen. Both of my examples come from the modern developed nations.

The first example comes from extreme household sanitation. Due to these anti-septic domestic environments a generation of humans has grown up with a far lesser proportion and variety of bacteria. A large fraction of these humans express extreme allergies and auto-immune diseases. The framework presented here suggests that this is caused by the immune system having far less to do, and being exposed to a far smaller range of pathogens than up to the previous generation of humans. In the same population it has been found that the presence of a pet like a dog or a cat during human infant-hood can improve the human's immune system.

The second example comes from extreme policing. Due to extreme measures, some cities in developed worlds have reduced violent crime to a level far below historical levels. This required additional enforcement staff and additional training. However, once the crime rate actually comes down, there is much less for the police to do. This may have led to some very high profile cases of over enforcement causing custodial deaths for relatively minor infractions.

For every organization there is an optimal level of rule breakers. This represents a dynamic equilibrium between providing a suitable deterrent to most members against breaking rules and actually having enough work for the rule enforcers to keep them engaged in appropriate rule enforcement. Thus, any large enough group of members must have some individuals who break any given rule- theft, murder, bribery, speed limits, paying taxes, and any other codified rule.

Aiming for zero rule breakers is as Utopian a dream as hoping for zero police.

11.2.6   Stem Cells and Long-Lived Animals

Multi-cellular animals have a tough strategic job. On the one hand they have to protect against all forms of smaller entities (bacteria, viruses and others) who have extremely short lifespans and evolve faster. On the other hand, any change they make in their cellular DNA has to propagate quickly across billions of cells so that internal police can still identify insiders and outsiders.

Cells make changes to their DNA constantly. They incorporate all kinds of fragments of DNA from the pathogens they face, from the food they eat, and the other cells they mate with. Reproduction is probably the most structured of these methods, but it happens rather infrequently- only once per generation. The others are more dynamic and risky, but can happen as frequently as needed. Bacteria are doing it, and so are plants and animals.

Suppose you were tasked with designing a method that would take the genetic code from a recent attacker and spread it all over the organization. How would you do it? Some cells live rather short lives. Blood cells and skin cells come to mind. Others live really long lives, like nerve cells.

One answer may be that you focus on the stem cells.

Stem cells are best known for their flexibility, since they can be coaxed to specialize into any other kind of cell in the body: muscle, skin, liver, anything. They have many other attributes. In any organ system they are the template from which other cells are created every day. There is an internal mechanism which maintains a ratio of stem cells to normal cells in the organ, creating more when there are too few, or allowing some to die off when there are too many. This balancing system has its limits, of course.

From here on it is all conjecture, or perhaps already established research that is not yet in the popular press.

To propagate a DNA "update" across the body there has to be a mechanism by which the immune system pushes these changes to the stem cells, and then allows the natural internal reproduction of cells to propagate these updates. Thus, at any point of time the most recent code is available within the immune system and then within the stem cells. The regular cells are probably one or two updates old.

This means that the longest-lived cells are the most vulnerable to attack. Perhaps glial cells surround nerve cells not only to electrically insulate them, but also to biologically protect them from pathogens. Perhaps that is one of the roles of the blood-brain barrier, which usually does not allow any cells to pass into the brain.

This mechanism arises from the necessity of competing against the attacks from faster evolving external entities.

11.2.7 Forest Fires and the Forestry Service

Once upon a time the Forest Service, which was tasked with preservation of national forests for the enjoyment of citizens, took a very aggressive attitude towards snuffing out forest fires. For a few decades this seemed to work. However they found that they had merely traded off a large number of frequent and small fires for a small number of rare but large and aggressive fires. They have currently decided on a path of frequent controlled burns. Time will reveal how this policy differs from the previous one.

Similarly, some economies have tried to eliminate employment uncertainty by legally banning bankruptcies, and also by owning large corporations (mining, infrastructure, "critical" industries). Over a couple of decades these public sector firms usually fall behind in efficiency due to lack of competitive pressures and finally end up costing the countries a rather large amount of their economic surplus. An extreme example of this comes from conventionally communist/socialist countries which have attempted some variant of this strategy.

Destruction and renewal is an integral part of every organization, at multiple levels. Every part of an organization changes, dies, and is replaced by new parts. An attempt to bring stability by artificially preventing death or change ends up weakening the larger organization.

11.3 Human Competition

11.3.1 The Marathon

The early history of Greek city states was full of battles between these states. For reasons related to geography and inadequate administrative technologies, these cities could not join together in any cohesive manner. However, they shared the same language and culture (although there are always variations in dialect and icons), and followed similar rules of engagement in battle.

During a battle between one of these states and the Persian Empire, a foot soldier ran a long distance without any stops to communicate a vital bit of information to the leaders, and died of exhaustion after completing the task. This was widely admired among all the peoples of these city-states.

During a period of relative calm these states decided to get together to complete on the basis of martial skills and signal their strength to each other, instead of using these skills directly in battle. Wrestling, archery, javelin throwing and many other skills were exercised. Along with these, the skill of running the same distance that the foot soldier had run was also incorporated, and called the marathon. There were shorter races too, which depended upon speed and strength. But the marathon was unique in its requirement of endurance. The winners of these competitions (all men in those days) had a lot of fame, wealth and women visited upon them.

Many generations later the technologies of war and administration had changed far beyond what the original group of city states could imagine. Longer wars were fought, over much wider geographies, with far greater casualties and losses. Yet, once again, in a period of relative calm the nations that fought these wars decided to bring back the original competitions of wrestling, archery, javelin throwing, and also the marathon. However, while these were still tests of individual skill and endurance, they were no longer relevant to the battlefield. Fame wealth and women continued to be visited upon the winners of these competitions. Since these skills were no longer relevant to the battlefield, women too participated in these competitions, and fame, wealth and men were visited upon these winners.

11.3.2   Luxury Collections and Pieces of Art

How do multi-billionaires compete? After a point, the practical things we can buy are no longer accurate gauges of individual wealth. In fact, determining net worth is itself a guessing game, no matter what "Top 100 Richest" lists would have us believe.

The extra space beyond your average ten-thousand square foot mansion is probably used to house armies of maintenance staff, or to provide services that can be obtained much cheaper down the block at the local shops. Many other toys, like planes and boats are probably owned through corporations and used as much for business as for personal enjoyment.

Thus, much of the competition between multi-billionaires is through collections- antiques, art, cars, perhaps companies and brands. There is no functional reason for some paintings to be worth hundreds of millions of dollars. These and other luxury collectibles are merely the objects of competitive display between billionaires. It would be so plebeian to merely compare net worth numbers.

Billionaires compete in other ways as well- who can donate the most to charity, whose influence among politicians is the greatest (although that has functional benefits as well), and many others.

11.4   Social Systems

11.4.1   The Lion and the Lamb

Various religious texts talk about a world in which the predator and the prey either sleep peacefully next to each other, or drink at the same watering hole. Generalized, it means that in the ideal organization each member is equal, with no regard to their inherent strength, wealth or status, and they have to both follow the same rules.

An intriguing example of this principle (and indeed many others) is usually very nicely available for us to interpret- the traffic conditions on roads.

One can argue that the best overall consumption of gasoline at traffic lights would be to allow the heaviest vehicles to proceed without stopping, since they take the most energy to bring back up to speed. In fact, as a historical snapshot, in the town of Kanpur, India (during the 1980s when I went to college there), this seemed to be the rule in force. Heavily laden trucks and larger vehicles hardly stopped, cars and motorcycles worked around them, and pedestrians and bicycles stopped the most, or wove their way around all heavier vehicles. The major exception, of course, was the category of animal-pulled carts and wagons, where everyone worked with the time required for the minders to get these animals to follow commands. Let us call this the "natural" system, since it does not require rules, or training. It is robust to interruptions and incidents, and is very flexible.

On the other hand, in the small town of Durham, North Carolina, the unmanned traffic light is the final word. Even in the middle of the night, with clear visibility for half a mile in every direction, almost everyone stands at a deserted red light till it turns green. In busier times a pedestrian needs to merely stand at a crossing in order to have a heavy tractor-trailer grind to a halt. This is thoroughly inefficient, in terms of energy and gas mileage. But those are the rules, and everyone follows them. We can call this the "artificial" system, since it depends upon rules (which often differ by country), and requires training for everyone[2].

The natural system is robust- it can deal with poorly maintained roads, the introduction of a new class of objects (e.g. cows), a vehicle breakdown, and many other unpredictable events. The artificial system, on the other hand, is very fragile, unable to han-

---

[2]This is not to say that the artificial traffic system is anything more than a temporary agreement among drivers. You have to look no further than the congested cities of Boston or Los Angeles to find examples where larger fractions of people break the rules. Or for that matter, in Durham in an accident-induced stoppage during rush hour on the I-40. The hungry lion is always tempted.

dle raccoon and deer venturing on the road, or a fender bender.

Yet the overall objective of transportation is probably handled better by the artificial system. It requires much less thinking by drivers, and allows far greater speeds. It also does require more training and physical maintenance. And both the Ford sedan and the Lamborghini sports car must abide by the speed limit (theoretically), although the latter may get to that speed quite a few seconds faster.

There is nothing sadder than seeing a finely-tuned performance car move slowly through congestion in a chaotic traffic system.

11.4.2 Breaking Rules- The "Jugaad" and "Guanxi" Fallacy

In the past couple of decades a lot of attention has been directed to the two ways in which entrepreneurs from India and China work in their own countries. This is, of course, from the point of view of German, American and other Western business executives who are frustrated in their attempts to conduct business in the way that they are used to. This bewilderment at how things actually work in a different cultural context is nothing new- if we go back a few more years, it was bewilderment at the Japanese system, to take one example.

As a brief introduction, "Jugaad" is the Indian attitude that one must "get it done". It is heart-warming to see young students learn how to solve engineering problems using old bicycle parts and other junkyard or garbage heap finds, or building musical instruments out of discarded boxes. It is also used to get business executives to think outside the box, and works great as an innovation workshop.

Similarly, "Guanxi" is the Chinese term for your own personal network, or connections. This can be used to get things done as well. When something novel is being attempted, or rules are ambiguous, then using personal connections to establish credibility can certainly get the work progressing.

Both of these ideas (innovative thinking and personal connections) are, of course, present in every country. Nowadays many high schools try to teach students how to be creative and mix the hard sciences with art. Business schools in the US teach their students how to establish connections and understand the need from the other party's point of view.

Yet, in the system analysis, both of these methods suffer from significant flaws when applied everywhere.

"Jugaad", when applied everywhere in a business context, signals a deliberate lack of adherence to rules. Similarly "Guanxi" denotes a lack of effort in creating rules. Both of these systems end up weakening the system. In the extreme, both of these systems have often led down the slippery slope into corruption and bribery. Ironically, it is not bribery if there are no rules against it, but I digress.

A society, an economy, or any system depends upon the individual rule-protester. This is a special kind of rule-breaker who does something that should be considered individually costly. When faced with a situation where they see that the "law is an ass", they can take two actions. First, they can break the law, or skirt around it. Or, second, they can spend much more of their own time getting signatures and support in order to petition a change in the law. In most cases the first action "gets it done" at a much lower cost of time and effort. Yet, these individuals persist and get the law changed. It is better for society, but worse for the individual in the short term.

This is what "Jugaad" and "Guanxi" miss out on- the evolution of the system. While this appears worse for the individual in the short term, if a large number of individuals focus their energy on making small parts of the system better for everyone, then it is a win for the system. This is, of course, extremely expensive. It requires a socialization of individuals from a young age to believe in following laws and rules, and also having the courage and belief to protest and change them when they feel that the rule is not working any more.

11.5 Business

11.5.1 The Hollywood Studio System

When the new technology of making moving pictures found itself embraced by the population as a method of entertainment, many economic and artistic questions faced the creators and organizers. By their nature, movies are artistic creations that are also subject to the laws of the marketplace. They compete with each other for the attention of the population, and there is indeed a winner-takes-all flavor to the outcomes.

Over these early decades of the industry there came to be a template for an organization that was called the Hollywood big studio. It involved an extensive system from the beginning of the creative process to the end delivery to the audience, that is, a vertically integrated system. Authors, actors, directors, musicians, editors, producers and movie theater operators- all joined this, even if it was not uniformly loved, and even if many unfair, exploitative and discriminatory practices were present. The reason for this aggregation of interests was simple: art is a brutal mistress. You are only as good as your last hit. Since even the most successful hits did not sustain revenue longer than a year, artistic and economic burnout was the norm before the big studio system emerged.

Provided you could get into it and stay loyal, a big studio offered an individual more stability than trying to make it alone. As the big studios emerged, there were indeed fewer and fewer opportunities left for the solo practitioner. Getting in was not easy either. You not only had to practice your craft of the flavor preferred by the big studios, but also had to get lucky. Thus, actors had to have conventional movie star looks, writers had to pen conventionally popular stories, composers had to orchestrate the right kind of scores, and so on. In various niches there still existed experimental and art films, but commercially and in terms of audience reach, they were almost an afterthought.

Each theater operator (often owned by the studios) ran movies exclusively from the big studio that it belonged to. Any independent operator had to take a bundle of movies to run. These included potential hits, as well as other not so successful films. This had the effect of averaging out the revenue from the films. This also provided the scale to the studio to run some parts of the operations more efficiently. Over time consolidation led to a few very large studios which operated on this business model.

This system was a victim of its own success when policy makers determined that it restricted choice, and applied anti-trust laws to repeal the end-to-end ownership of the movie making enterprise.

Today we are once again in a vast open space where there is little structure and a very winner-takes-all flavor to movie-like media conceptualization, production and distribution. Within this we have almost-closed vertically integrated systems like Netflix, Amazon and others.

11.5.2 Business Incubators and Exit Plans

One area of business activity with an unusually high mortality rate is the area of entrepreneurship, particularly in dynamic modern economies (it is the most visible and commented upon in the area of high-tech and life science entrepreneurship). This hyper activity is made possible by a combination of many structural factors, including a vibrant acquisition culture, availability of capital, robust property rights, and permissive bankruptcy laws. Startup survival, defined as being in existence a year (or five) is estimated to be less than 10%, and may be as low as 1% depending upon the industry.

Under such brutal conditions, it is natural that both the startups and the founders and employees of these startups are always searching for organizations that make this roller coaster a bit more stable.

One such form of organization is the business incubator. A business incubator provides a common space for startups, and may take startup equity in exchange for rents. Some incubators provide additional services such as mentorship and various shared services and specialized resources. A startup must endure a selective membership process, and be evaluated for potential on a number of criteria before being allowed into an incubator.

Investing time and money in these startups makes sense for the incubator since they are then able to aggregate the scarce resources needed for entrepreneurial success and leverage them across multiple startups, each of which represents a single roll of the dice where the chances of individual success are low, but the rewards are high when success does happen.

For the startups this represents a reasonable trade-off of some equity in return for a slightly increased chance for success. This slight increase comes from the availability of resources and expertise that they would not have been able to procure on their own, as well as from the additional oversight and mentorship of the incubator owners.

For the founders and employees the incubator represents a network of opportunities that they can leverage after the current startup attempt fails. Upon failure the startup breaks apart back into the constituent founders and employees who now have to figure out what to do next. In some cases founders and employees may simultaneously pursue more than one startup opportunity, hence providing some cushion against the sudden dissolution of any specific startup.

At the next level of organization, each incubator also competes with other incubators for capital, and for startups to join them.

11.5.3   Management Consultants

Management consultants (the large four consultant firms in the US) are organizations which help other organizations address business issues, determine strategy and develop new capabilities. Most of them will analyze the context and make recommendations, and some may also implement the recommendations. Considered from the organizational perspective, they are a very important part of the competitive and evolutionary narratives in the lives of corporate organizations.

While the big four consulting firms are the most polarizing, our discussion applies to smaller consulting firms as well, in a toned down manner. Established consulting firms are able to charge high fees and provide expertise in almost all areas of business. They are highly favored by large corporations, and not so much by smaller or newer firms (even large newer firms).

Management consultants are often unfairly painted in a bad light. Although they are considered indispensable by large corporations, they are also stereotyped as those who borrow your watch to tell you the time. They put fresh graduates into demanding roles, traveling all across the country and the world to gather context and data that seniors use to craft their recommendations. The 5-year attrition rate is quite high, particularly when these junior consultants think about settling down.

The basic form of a consulting engagement depends heavily upon repeatability. If many firms in a specific industry are facing a business problem that they may not have the resources or capabilities to solve on their own, then this is the ideal condition for the entry of consulting services that can take one solution and apply it to those firms who are able to pay the fees. When most of these firms have completed the transformation, or the business context has made this specific engagement irrelevant, then the consultants move to the next repeatable need. Upgrading business processes, finding new partners in the business ecosystem (like supply chains, equipment suppliers, and distribution partners), modern ways to connect with customers- these are some common repeatable engagements.

From the organizational perspective, consider what happens when one deer develops a longer neck, giving it an advantage in reaching for leaves higher up in the tree. Instead of waiting a few generations before this genetic variant spreads across the entire herd, management consultants are able to cobble together a slightly larger neck for all the other deer in the herd who can pay the engagement fees. A human analogy would be cosmetic surgery for television, media and entertainment aspirants. They don't have to live with what nature and nurture gave them. Instead, they can shape their faces and bodies to conform to what gives them a better chance at success in the current popular looks.

Thus, management consultants are a way of propagating successful business innovations across an industry. In other words, they speed up evolution by intra-generational transfer of competitive advantages across firms. This is faster than the intergenerational DNA-based transfer of competitive advantage across cells and animals.

11.5.4 Business Disruption

The idea of disruption of business industries[3] has influenced business strategy for the past few decades. An important aspect of the process of disruption is the critical moment when technology improves enough to allow companies to easily provide the functional requirements of most customers. Before this moment companies compete on functional parameters. Some examples of functionality are raw horsepower for cars, processor and memory size for computers and other types of functionality.

There are dozens of industries where the market leaders before this transition lose out when the transition happens. Recently these ideas have come under criticism since they appear to no longer hold true[4]. The post-disruption scenario has not been explored adequately in his work or subsequent researchers. Part of the reason is that consulting expertise has focused on helping incumbent companies fight or slow the effect of disruption, while the approach of the disruptors has fallen on to venture capitalists and other funding entities who are looking to invest in the companies with hyper-growth potential.

The post-disruption landscape in an industry is confusing precisely because it is no longer along functional dimensions. The original work on disruption mentions that the new leaders compete on "other" dimensions like customer service. This is misleading since it assumes that the competitive dimension will continue to be a functional one. That is true only in some cases.

Disruption is very likely if the initial competitive dimension is functional. It fails to be as impactful if the competitive dimension

---

[3]Dr. Clayton Christensen's book "The Innovator's Dilemma" has influenced business since it was published in the mid-1990s.

[4]This is ironic, since the publication of Dr. Christensen's ideas now allows companies to try to plan for this transition.

has evolved to be artistic (as defined earlier, i.e. in-system or non-functional competitions). Companies built on stable brands like Apple, Coke, Nike and others leverage this in their strategic approach.

11.6   Nations, Governance, Economies

11.6.1   The Moonshot

In the 1960s, the two superpowers had already each developed a large stockpile of nuclear bombs along with the ballistic missile delivery systems needed to drop them on their intended targets. Unlike conventional weapons which could be field tested in various proxy wars in different parts of the world, nuclear weapons presented a riskier fallout, both politically and biologically (i.e. at different levels of organization).

The purpose of war is never to obliterate the enemy. It is to destabilize the enemy organization enough to be able to re-use parts of them in our system. In the past this incorporation happened with territorial annexation. Today this happens in the form of economic and trade integration. Thus, nuclear war is undesirable in that it offers no spoils to the victor[5].

Since nuclear war was not an attractive option, both parties needed to find an artistic competition through which to decide a winner. This competition needed to

- involve the technologies used in war but not be war itself (i.e. explicitly involve no death),

- present a goal which was not trivial and

- have no real economic or functional benefit to the winner, except to allow all participants to recognize a winner.

Both countries found the perfect competition. It was to land man on the moon.

---

[5]That does not mean it cannot happen, just that it is not that attractive.

The moonshot had all the characteristics of an in-system artistic competition, namely

- it used the same rockets and targeting systems that nuclear missiles used,

- it was used for a target that was quite challenging,

- it provided no real functional benefit (setting up a colony on the moon is still not economically feasible fifty years later).

All of us know how the story ends. In fact, this is one of the main arguments we can use against various conspiracy theories which claim that the moon landing was a hoax. If it were a hoax, nuclear war would have either already happened, or would have continued to be imminent.

The "social" benefits of winning the moonshot were real indeed. This was the point, arguably, at which it became clear that communism in its contemporary form was not a viable economic system. It still took two more decades for the wall to come down, and on a related note, for China to open up to trade. Even today there are still a few struggling holdouts to the old form of communism, but it is no longer viewed as an effective economic alternative to capitalism. (On a related note, the lack of a viable alternative weakens capitalism too.)

11.6.2 Communism, Capitalism and Economic Dynamism

Communism and capitalism have danced against each other for the past century. They have each evolved in response to the weaknesses and strengths of each other, and each has been implemented in different forms in different countries that have adopted them. The following discussion simplifies the nature of each in order to focus on the organizational differences between them.

From the economic perspective communism was conceived in response to two excesses of its times. The first was the unfettered power of some companies in successfully commercializing emerging technologies, and the second was the exploitation of many countries under the colonial system.

Communism explicitly makes all assets belong to the local collective, usually the village. Capitalism, on the other hand depends upon private property ownership, and the right to all value generated by that property. This has usually meant that a communist system ends up receiving only a part of the effort and initiative of its ordinary members. This is because when an individual's output is shared with "everybody", the effective tax rate approaches 100%.

Since any property belongs to "all", the communist system must figure out how to assign tasks and roles, as well as how to spread the value generated from all these assets. This has traditionally placed a large planning burden on the system and required an army of economists and statisticians to make any decision. This also means that any decision has to be of a minimum scope (usually large) and will take a certain time (usually long).

The communist system thus has to use collectivist thought and mild-to-heavy coercion to ensure a higher effort from its members. On a practical level it also meant that any non-collective enjoyment of the results of one's efforts can happen as long as it does not trigger the monitoring of the collective. This probably happened at all levels from the individual to the regional state.

Capitalism, on the other hand, allows the individual to own property and gain all the value from it, and periodically give to the collective taxes on this resulting value. This has the advantage of transparency in both the generated value and the tax share. Thus, while the individual has an incentive to work harder, this is tempered with questions about the purpose and usage of the taxes she pays.

For the system itself, at inception, a communist system has distinct advantages over a capitalist system. Even with a lower level of enthusiasm and participation from its members, the freedom to use almost all of the value they generate in return for basic necessities seems to provide the communist system with a larger surplus to work with. Additionally, a suitably structured indoctrination system (which every system has) can reduce the proportion of members who want to leave the system. Thus, at its beginning the communist system, usually created from its member's anger at an exploitative capitalist system gives it a huge advantage in both its members' participation and belief, as well as an almost complete surplus.

A large part of this initial surplus also comes from repressing the competitive drive in its members. In a capitalist system a large part of the economic activity is devoted to signaling status and ability between members. You don't need a Lamborghini for transportation alone. You don't need a 10,000 square feet mansion to merely sleep in at night.

The silencing of the competitive urge has a significant long-term effect on the economy. The additional modern capitalist institutions of a stock market and a thriving entrepreneurship culture allow the competitive duality of greed and fear to amplify the competitive urge to a higher level. It is analogous to a controlled explosion- a dangerous thing, certainly, but it is also the operating principle of a large number of modern machines.

The capitalist economy gains in the long term because it does not try to suppress the basic competitive nature of its members for any short-term gain in ease of governability of the system. This too needs significant resources in conditioning members to believe in the system, because in the short-term the life and death of startups and businesses imposes significant costs on members.

A third direction in which a population can be driven is towards asceticism or transcendence from material values, which is also encapsulated in religions similar to Buddhism. Both capitalism and communism require engaging with the world and continuing to work towards something. If the primary message in the system is that life and materialism are illusions, then in addition to reducing the competitiveness between individuals, it will also reduce their economic output quite significantly. This leaves the system considerably weaker relative to other non-transcendent systems, and hence susceptible to defeat against other systems. This is one of the reasons that many Buddhism-based kingdoms of the world were overrun when the young and energetic new Muslim faith arrived on their borders.

From the organizational point of view the mechanism used to unite members internally matters only because it can impact the strength of the organization when it has to compete or fight against other organizations. At an abstract level, no matter which religion and which economic philosophy the members follow, every day their organization must face off against other organizations in a competing system. A system may shrink from the slow loss of its most capable and competitive members, or it may lose when one day it find itself unable to use its knives against others with guns.

11.6.3 Monarchy, Democracy and Continuity in Political Systems

While the rules may work for you and me and the average member, they cannot be a prescription for whoever is at the top of a large system. For one, the leadership of the organization has to contend with the presence and strategies of other organizations, working on timescales greater than an individual member's lifetime or tenure. For another, all enforcement mechanisms have to converge somewhere (who polices the police, after all) [6].

The weakest moment in a traditional monarchy is the transition from one king to another. If the king is weak, then ambitious soldiers and provincial governors start jockeying for power long before the incumbent king is dead, and may indeed end up defeating and killing the previous king. If the king is strong today, then this process has to wait till the king is old and physically weakened.

A democracy is not much better, if indeed the only characteristic it has is that it elects leaders periodically. For the duration

---

[6]If this convergence of powers is with a member or group different from the nominal leadership, then it leads to instability in governance and continuity. An example of this is the rise and dominance of the Prætorian Guard in the Roman Empire from an elite corps of security escorts to the personal security detail of the emperors to becoming powerful enough to interfere in Roman politics.

of her rule, there is enormous operational freedom concentrated in the office and person of the elected leader . More often than not, this power is used to consolidate her status and power, as well as weaken any potential opposition. This is not fundamentally different from what a monarch does. The eventual transition point in a democracy with no countervailing checks and balances is just as disruptive as it is in a monarchy.

What gives rise to a stable political system? It can trade off smoother day-to-day governance using more powerful leadership by kicking the can down the road to when there has to be the eventual leadership transition. On the other hand, it can choose a slightly more chaotic governance by enforcing more frequent leadership change. To prevent the leadership itself from sabotaging this scheme there also has to be some form of separation of powers.

There cannot be effective separation of powers with just two centers of power. It is very easy for one power to strategize around or work with one other power. One could argue whether it is effective with just three sources of power, but it is definitely better than just two. The executive, legislative and judiciary branches are considered to be the three separate sources of power in order keep each other in balance. One can also argue that the religious and community organizations, the business community and the media are other sources of power. Finally, the local police and armed forces, the intelligence services, and bureaucracy are also present in this debate. It is tempting to consider the analogy between these systems and various organ systems in a multi-cellular body, i.e. skeletal, muscular, digestive, circulatory, endocrine, nervous and others.

Irrespective of their economic system some countries have effectively one source of power. They combine into one body what is considered nominally three separate sources of power in the form of the elected leader , the rule-making body, and the judges. These countries do not implode and collapse simply because they do not have a separation of powers or term limits. There are other less visible sources of power which may keep them balanced. Even if all power were with one body, the benefits can be visible immediately. However the risks from such a choice are not immediate.

They happen at the time of leadership transition.

11.6.4   Economic Leadership vs Catching Up

For many years after the great wars USA was far ahead of the others in terms of its economic strength. Perhaps this was because it was on the victorious side, and perhaps because it was because in spite of suffering large casualties in the war the homeland was far from the active theaters of war.

After the other countries recovered from the destruction and tragedies of the great wars they wanted to recover the strength of their economies. These countries were all very diverse. They were from both sides of the wars, and followed different economic systems.

Japan chose the idea of close coordination between its government, its banks and its businesses in order to focus on strategic priorities and invest heavily in certain industries. Since the target was to mimic the imitable strengths of the leading country, this worked for about two decades from about 1970. This was about 5 or 6 cycles of investment with positive economic returns from each cycle of investment.

This also built a sense of confidence in Japan that they could do it. After all, they had done this many times, and come out ahead each time. However, as they came closer to the economic scope of the US, they did not realize the risks in following a copy strategy when the target is not quite that far ahead. Finally, in 1990 it was clear that the previous cycle of investment was turning sour. A lot of the money that the country had invested in the last economic bet would not be recovered.

Since they had not built other complementary skills of economic transparency, and since it was important to the national leaders to appear strong, they pretended for a very long time that these bets were still economically viable. They also did not have a culture of acceptance of bankruptcy and mass layoffs. As a result, for about thirty years this economy, though not poor, has had almost no growth at all. The bad investments are still on the books of their banks, and there is still no appetite to change the culture of business and accountability.

This story would be an interesting historical one, except for the fact that a similar plot line is being played out with another country as we write these words, but with even less transparency and openness than in Japan in the 1960s-1990s.

China has applied a similar directed model of development from the mid-1980s till today. This has been spectacularly successful. In fact, from 2002 to 2012 China's GDP increased from about $2 trillion to $10 trillion. In comparison, the US economy is almost $20 trillion, and that of Japan is about $14 trillion. After 2012, however, China has had a number of crises, beginning with over-investment in real estate, to volatility in the stock market, and other issues. In most cases the Chinese government has responded by direct intervention in the markets, and by channeling the message in the media to suit its purpose. In recent months it has doubled down on its path by elevating the status and power of its premiere.

My conjecture is that at the center of it is the same dilemma that faced Japan in the late 1980s.

Suppose you have one trillion dollars that you wish to invest in the next big thing. Societal expectation may force your hand-you need continued economic growth. What will you do?

If you were Japan in 1988, or China in 2016, you have behind you an enviable track record of the previous thirty years. You started with a small amount, perhaps $50 billion. Over a series of planned moves coordinated with your national banks, economic departments and private enterprise, you have succeeded in each of your last ten moves. Over that time you have built this corpus into more than a trillion dollars. If you have also played the political game, you have the support of the majority of the country, and the positive expectations of everyone behind you. Why try something new that may or may not work? You follow the same process that has worked for thirty years. You call upon your best team to make a prediction, and provided it is politically feasible, you make your trillion dollar bet. In many cases, you also mould the political system to make it feasible.

11.6.5 The US Economic Engine

On the other hand, if you are the USA, at any point of time in the recent decades, far before you get to a trillion, the first question people will ask is why does the government have so much money to spare? After a very noisy tax reform, you will no longer have anything more than a billion or two. Although no individual has a trillion dollars in the US, many individuals have billions. So let us begin with that.

The US method, driven by greed and the presence of capital markets works like this. First you hand out about $25,000 to thousands of founder groups. Let us assume you have 10,000 such founders. Note that this is after they have spent about $5,000 of their own money to gain some traction. Let us count that too in the final cost, along with another 10,000 founders who lost their $5,000 with nothing to show for it. Thus, at this point we have already spent (20,000 X $5,000) + (10,000 X $25,000) which is $350 million.

At this point, however, the game gets very difficult. Only one in ten make it to the next level, where they are now rewarded with a million dollars to work with. So, after spending $350 million to test out 20,000 ideas we now put in some serious money. $1 billion goes into the 1,000 best ideas. However, this is not the end of the story. Only a 100 of these are serious ideas with national scale, and so we spend $10 million on each, i.e. another $1 billion.

At the end of the year we have spent $2.35 billion dollars to get a hundred solid ideas with national potential. The other 19,900 groups are forgiven their losses, and are free to refine their ideas and try again next year. This is in fact such a profitable endeavor that the government gets no chance to play the game. Many wealthy individuals (of the order of $100 million) invest a significant part of their wealth in venture capital funds.

The US government does not make trillion dollar bets. They set up the business environment with permissive bankruptcy laws and well-functioning capital markets so that there is always an army of individuals searching for the next big thing, with many prototypes ready to hit the ground running. For every startup which has succeeded in the last ten years there have been innumerable variants tried before when perhaps the technology was not ready, or the consumers were not ready, or their own ideas were too vague to be actionable.

This process is not attractive to politicians or bureaucrats looking to make a big mark. It is almost a daily grind, leaving a lot of collateral damage since the chances of success are very low. Yet it seems to be the only way that works when the direction forward is not clear. It is the only process that ensures that the economic leader continues to generate new ideas to build the next set of large companies and employers.

In a way, this is a structured way of creating an environment where competition ensures the survival of this year's best ideas. But the other ideas do not die. They are modified and entered into the competition again. This is evolution at a breakneck speed, where prototyping and piloting a specific form of an idea or innovation takes the place of DNA and populations.

Everybody can see what the US does in this area. It is no secret. Numerous academics, practitioners, wealthy people and policy makers study this and try to replicate that in various parts of the US. Many foreigners study the system, and try to replicate that in their nations. The elements that are difficult to replicate are the capital markets, extreme transparency for bad business news, social and legal acceptance of bankruptcy, and an independent legal system holding all sides accountable. Many foreign wealthy individuals and nations prefer investing in the US ecosystem rather than try to seriously replicate this in their home locations.

11.6.6   The Last Word

While it is inconceivable that the US will exclusively retain this vibrant economic engine forever, so far no other economy has come close to developing a similar startup engine. Eventually, of course, this too shall pass.

What must be necessary for this to end? Will it be a nation that directs and plans the activities of its citizens? Will it be a nation that uses national forms of all emerging social media and communication technologies to better assess the feasibility of implementing its plans? Will it be a nation that suppresses dissent so effectively that its citizens may not even know that they cannot think certain thoughts? Will it be a nation that commits itself to the vision and plans of one human or one (small) group of thought leaders? No matter how implausible we think these national strategies are, every nation tries to implement these whenever a new technology arises that hold promise. This often translates to real gains over a decade or two, which is often longer than how far most humans look. As we have discussed, each of these national strategies translates to a rejection of small-scale strategy change. But that comes at a cost of uncontrollable disruptive change at some time in the future.

The US system is based partly on believing that it is better to have structured and controlled dissonance and debate, structured competition for products and ideas. Yet these take time to self-correct, and are indeed quite fragile systems. There is no guarantee that the time it takes to self-correct is short enough to regain any temporarily lost leadership on the world stage without falling too far behind. There is never a stable balance between the need for competition (to stay vibrant) and the drive towards protected monopolies (leading to stagnation). The siren song of temporary stability appeals to each of us. None of us wants to lose our job today.

11.7 Other Philosophical Musings

11.7.1 Evolution and Beauty

Ever since the publication of Darwin's thoughts on evolution a debate has emerged in the biology community about the nature and purpose of beauty (the debate precedes Darwin's thesis, and took on modern terminology at that point). Darwin himself struggled with the idea of beauty in the world[7]. Beauty exists, but why? Recent debates have not reached any conclusion on the purpose of beauty. However, in our framework beauty is critical to competition, as well as the organizational complexity of the universe.

If we explore the idea of competition from the perspective of reducing the risk of death and couple it with the need to still compete, we have shown that non-functional competition emerges as the main solution. This explains the presence of beauty in our lives and in the world around us. Beauty exists in animals, insects, plants and all other entities which compete. That is the main mechanism that allows the world to self-organize into more complex levels.

We exist because atoms are beautiful, molecules are beautiful, single cells are beautiful, multi-cellular animals and plants are beautiful, humans are beautiful, and so are religions, countries, companies and industry groups. They all compete, and most of the time they compete on beauty.

11.7.2   I, Change

Every moment that I exist, my atoms arise out of a foam of subatomic particles that come into being and annihilate each other with energies far greater than everything mankind has harnessed so far.

Every moment I exist my molecules are gaining and losing atoms in a continuous dance inside my body. My body also adds molecules from the environment and loses molecules to the environment at an equally frenetic pace.

Every day I exist old cells are dying and new cells are being born in my body. Every day I eat plants and animals and incorporate their cells and molecules into my body.

I am not the same physical being that I was last year, last month or a minute ago. Yet I consider myself to be a continuous human being. I am temporary and I am permanent.

---

[7]"The sight of a feather in a peacock's tail, whenever I gaze at it, makes me sick!", in Darwin's letter to Asa Gray on 3rd April 1860.

When I die, another human being will continue to do the tasks I do today, assuming that my group still exists. If my group disbands before I die, I will attempt to find another group.

Chapter 12

Commandments for the Inside

After the parables, let us consider some sets of representative commandments for different entities. These sets of rules depend upon where the entity is in relation to the organization.

Our attempt will be to craft some rules that will apply to entities across many layers. These sets are also incomplete by design, and are always open to debate.

Consider first, those entities who follow all the rules of the organization and completely believe in them. Of all the past attempts at similar rule schematics for these members, the ones with the highest longevity must clearly be rule books for "good" people. "Good" people belong to an organization and are expected to uphold the rules of the community. While such rules are not exclusively the domain of religion, they have traditionally been very close to the core of religious values. In modern times with the rise of nation-states, citizenship also comes with a rule book for good behavior. This framework is not for them- the commandments and the rule books already tell them all that they need to know. In fact, if we tell the good citizen that the rules she follows are rather arbitrary, and that there are many other groups of good people who do not follow the same rules, then the good citizen may be more inclined to grab a pitchfork and attack us.

We will list a few such rules, aiming to be neither accurate, nor complete. We take this approach so as to not waste your time, since we consider these to be well documented, with numerous examples, and lengthy thoughtful debates in religion and constitutional law about the merits and costs of subtle variations and interpretations of such codes, beginning from Hammurabi to modern religions and nation states. Additionally, we know that our knowledge of these sets of laws is close to zero, and we urge you to find your local expert in these matters. We will restrict ourselves to those aspects of the rules which pertain to organizational consequences.

12.1 Rule 1: A Member will Not Kill

Killing is the one activity that should be explicitly forbidden, since reducing the risk of death is the central driver for creation of organizations. Actually, modify that slightly- a member will not kill other members. If you are particularly generous, you can modify this to a member will not kill other members of her own organization, or members of similar nearby organizations.

In context, killing may mean something much less than what it reads as. In sports competitions it may mean any action which disables the opponent from competing in future competitions- as an example, by injury or threat of injury.

For all members to continue to believe in the organization, any killing or attempt to kill must carry a penalty. It is a matter of debate whether that penalty can be death, which is itself a form of killing. For example, during a game, if a player deliberately injures another player with the intent to injure and eliminate the other player, the penalty may be suspension from a number of future games, or in egregious cases, permanently.

Killing non-members is a strange activity, and used as a last resort. It seems that it is generally preferable to try and convert non-members, rather than kill them. However, direct conversion attempts are not polite, and threats to kill are not polite either. Perhaps in earlier times it was more common to kill, and to use the threat of killing to achieve conversions. Today we often use more subtle tools to enforce conversion to the systems we care about.

12.2 Rule 2: A Member will Fight Threats

While a member may not kill other members, this cannot be extended to members of other organizations. Other organizations have members who are often almost the same as members of the home organization, which creates a common dilemma. On the one hand these other members may be attractive as converts and new members, but on the other hand they may also want to do the same and take away members from the home organization.

Thus every organization builds in training to carefully identify members by their affiliation to the home organization, and also to identify members of other organizations. Ironically, members who are a bit more different trigger no threat response, but the closer a member is to the home organization members, the greater the "danger". This is a delicate and difficult balance.

12.3 Rule 3: A Member will Follow Rules (list here)

This part of the commandments for members usually consists of a set of rules, sometimes general and assumed self-explanatory, and sometimes presented in much detail. Examples of rules include prohibitions against theft, unauthorized procreative activities, misrepresentation, and so on.

Rules are a fundamental part of easing the interactions between diverse members. Rules guarantee that behavior learned in one part of the organization can still be used when a member moves to another part. It is only because of rules enacted in the form of two yellow lines painted in the middle of the road that I am willing to drive my car towards another car coming almost exactly at me at a combined lethal speed of a hundred miles per hour.

Without diving into a discussion of rule-breakers (see Chapter 6), all members in an organization must follow and enforce rules. This implies that beyond a certain size the organization must devote specialized resources to rule creation, modification and enforcement. This constitutes an overhead which has a natural tendency to increase over time and which will choke the organization if left untended.

Many organizations have attempted to handle complexity in the rule book by splitting it up into a small set of principles which are considered stable over time, and a larger set of operating rules that are subject to frequent addition, modification and pruning. The United States constitution takes a similar approach. On the other hand, the Indian constitution does not separate out the stable from the modifiable, and has had an amendment almost every year after it was created.

12.4 Rule 4: A Member will Enforce and Propagate This Message

A very important part of the membership is a strong belief in the organization. There is always a variation in the degree of belief in the core values of the organization, which may be primarily about the implicit norms in the organization. The larger the organization, the greater the chances for belief variations, for a given set of communication tools.

Thus a part of the time and effort of the organization and its members has to be spent in discovering and merging variations in beliefs. This usually takes the form of a commandment, since otherwise it takes a lower priority to life in general. To ensure that it is followed each organization uses a set of interlocking beliefs which reinforce each other in terms of potential or actual rewards and punishment.

As an example, various studies of business firms have found that successful organizations foster a deep belief in the products and services of the organization. Various large tech firms follow a form of indoctrination that may be likened to a cult, and in earlier times long-lasting tobacco companies believed in their product to such a deep extent that it may almost have been impossible to work there unless one also smoked cigarettes.

While most of this message propagation effort is spent internally, many organizations also reward external dissemination. Businesses, countries, religions- all ask their members to spread the word to different degrees.

12.5   Blind Spots

What many existing rules fail to specify are the mechanisms by which the organization stays healthy. That means that at every level of interaction there must be a healthy competition between groups. If any particular context within an organization does not have competition, it increases the risk that that context will not keep up with internal and external changes, and be a weak link for the organization.

Another aspect that many rules often fail to address is the related topic of life and death of groups within the organization. Each group within an organization does evolve, by changing its governance, its members and its interactions with other groups. But that can only carry it a certain distance from its birth.

This is the basis for explicit rules and governing approaches, like term limits for elected office, for keeping government out of business, and even for elections, for that matter.

12.6   How to Kill a Large Organization

We have had situations in the past where even though one organization has nominally defeated another, the vanquished does not die because its members have a set of beliefs that are self-supporting and cannot be easily replaced with another set from the victor organization. Colonialism provides many examples, from South Africa to India. One can argue that a similar dynamic is playing out between capitalism and communism.

In such cases the only way to proceed is to first disbar the defeated members from propagating the old message, and to simultaneously weaken each belief through re-education and advertising. This does not make it easy or quick.

Each colonial power attempted to do this in their colonies by first demeaning various elements of native religion. Simultaneously they created educational institutions which promoted a non-religious form of education, along with missionaries who came in to fill the vacuum left in the population from demolished religions. While this succeeded to an extent, the task was not complete when the entire economic philosophy behind colonialism came to an end with the two great wars.

The similarity of the internal rules of large organizations notwithstanding, organizations do fight each other. Other than the quirks of some genetic material, there is no essential difference between the skin cells of two mammals, say the zebra and the lion. Yet one of them hunts, kills and consumes the other. Similarly, the actual differences between the rules of competing organizations are minor in the larger scheme of things, but take on an overpowering importance for the members themselves.

Chapter 13

Commandments for the Top

Leaders often live in an affluent world. But their world is very fickle, and leadership can be snatched away at any moment. While they are expected to be knowledgeable about the nature of the organization they helm, their personal history is often a pampered one in the heart of the organization. Leaders with capable lieutenants and experienced mentors may still be able to provide some leadership.

While not as widespread as manuals for members, there are many manuals for leaders as well. Many of these are probably notes and techniques passed down by hand to those leaders who are willing to learn. After all, one of the greatest challenges for an organization is the training of second-generation potential leaders. Two treatises come to mind- Machiavelli's "The Prince", and Chanakya's "Artha Shashtra" ("The Study of Wealth", loosely translated, but broader, covering govenment, law and other topics), both of which attempt to explain to the prince how to rule.

The challenge for a leadership manual is quite stark- while on the one hand the leader represents the best of the organization to its members, on the other hand she also represents the organization to other organizations and lone wolves. The leader has to be two-faced.

What makes a particular set of rules for leaders better than another? It is quite simple- organization survival. Thus, one can easily imagine a stressful environment where any and all of these commandments should be violated if it helps the organization survive. A leader can and must abandon or sacrifice loyal members to that end. A leader must serve the organization, not individual members.

Here is our attempt to craft an incomplete set of commandments for the capable leader .

13.1 Rule 1: A Member-Leader will Nurture Followers

The leader represents the face of the organization to its members. She must represent the most exalted of the dreams of the entities, and a role model for all to aspire to. This is a very public role, and it is doubtful if any mortal can completely fill this job description.

Thus, among the tasks of the leader are the following

- Reward those who are the actual producers,

- Recognize those who are the most conformant of the organizational rules,

- Nurture internal minor leadership for various internal activities,

- Motivate all members to address any external threats to the organization,

- Uphold the rules and rule-enforcers (i.e. police) particularly in times of stress,

- Uphold the rule modification process (if that exists),

In short, the leader must lead during peace, and during war.

13.2 Rule 2: A Member-Leader will Nurture Rule-Breakers and Encourage Rule Modification

Rule modification is a critical part of organizational evolution when it is possible to modify rules[1]. This constitutes a powerful tool for intra-generational modification of organizations, allowing adaptations and efficiencies to spread at much faster rates.

For organizations where rule modification is possible, the leader must actively seek out rule breakers, understand the reasons for these infractions, and figure out mechanisms that will use these to drive rule modification. The animal body actively seeks out the code from pathogens like bacteria and viruses and incorporates their DNA into its own. Every human genome contains an archaeological imprint of every epidemic its ancestors have survived over the past millennia. This allows for a better response to future attacks even from evolved pathogens since the animal body has a template, albeit old, from which to start crafting a counter strategy.

Human organizations encompass a great variety of individuals and behaviors. For an organization whose sole purpose is to sell bagels the rule book necessarily concerns itself primarily with following the laws of the land, and with selling bagels in the most profitable manner. If the environment changes and customers buy bagels differently, the survival of the organization depends upon nurturing and propagating non-traditional forms of bagels. Since this does not happen overnight, any organization which obsessively enforces rules will be left with a far smaller pool of variations from which to start experimenting.

---

[1]There are many contexts where that is not possible, for instance the basic chemistry of bio-molecules does not allow much modification if the environmental conditions like temperature and pressure continue to hold in the same range as before. On the other hand, it is interesting to note that many biochemical processes have persisted even after the external environments have changed, allowing the same biochemical template to exist on land, in freshwater, saltwater, and miles into the depths of the ocean.

A locally owned burger shop can add salads to its menu far quicker than a large national burger chain. The national burger chains with the most franchise restaurants have long operating manuals specifying every aspect of operations. This allows the individual franchises little room to experiment. Thus they must also wait for customer preference changes to reach a critical fraction before they can react and change (slowly).

13.3 Rule 3: A Member-Leader will Break Rules Outside

In order to ensure the survival and success of her organization the leader must be willing to break any of the rules that apply internally. This represents the inherent tension in leadership.

If all that the leader does is to represent the best aspirations of the members, then that is a rather weak leader . That is only one half of her role. The other half is representing the organization when dealing with the outside.

Dealing with the outside of the organization may involve dealing with non-member entities and it may also involve dealing with other organizations. In the absence of any particular structure or past interactions the leader must assume that these outside entities are most likely antagonistic to the values and goals of the organization.

This is a difficult task for anyone who has led a completely rule-abiding life before becoming the leader . Such an entity would make many mistakes in her dealing with the outside if her decisions are driven by her internal instincts. Unless the organizations themselves are part of a super-organization in the next layer, the perfect member is the worst leader .

This may be a difficult reality for regular rule-abiding members to accept. Often members cannot understand the necessity of choosing a leader who is remarkably imperfect (according to their rule-abiding sensibilities). If the leader herself is not that bad, often their advisers and inner circle may be abhorrent. If the rule-breaking leadership circle additionally encourages rule-abiding among citizens then it may seem that the world is upside down.

Yet breaking rules outside the organization is an essential attribute of the leader , and perhaps the most important role. Otherwise the organization incurs unnecessary risk.

13.4 Rule 4: A Member-Leader will Ensure Organization Continuity Beyond Her Demise

A leader must ensure that the organization endures after she retires, dies, is deposed or hits term limits. Although infrequent, this is one of the weakest points in time for any organization. If the strategy of the organization is closely linked to the leader , then her replacement may also end up drastically changing the organization's strategy. If the new strategy is crafted from inexperience then the organization may be at a competitive disadvantage.

Many forms of human organizations suffer from this. Monarchies have traditionally suffered from contentious leadership transitions when princes have often gone to war to establish their right to the throne. Similarly charismatic CEOs often lead the organization down a strategic path that is uniquely suited to their skills and preferences, making their successor's jobs much more difficult. This is made worse by the common flaw of purging the organization of any developing strong challengers.

Unlike the cells of an animal, members of human organizations do not share identical DNA. Hence there is always the temptation of favoring those who are similar to themselves. This temptation extends to leaders too, and a weak leader may work to get her genetic successors to take over the leadership after her, and to consolidate power. Yet the human organization survives better if power is balanced across at least three or four groups/institutions.

161

13.5 Do We Need a Leader?

The final thought on organizations and member-leaders is to ask whether organizations need leaders at all. After all, an organization can create a mechanism by which a common set of rules are agreed upon and enforced, along with a process to modify it based on the dynamics of member interactions. Enforcing internal rules is not the primary role of the leader , even though they may assist in it.

We do not need leaders if an organization exists by itself (which happens, but very rarely). The primary role of the leader is to monitor the environment and implement strategy changes if they estimate that the environment warrants it. In that sense, the leader is also an evolutionary mechanism for the organization to adapt. Since most of the uncertainty for an organization comes from other organizations similar to itself[2], the role of the leader is to determine how to handle this and other external uncertainties.

---

[2]We have mentioned this aspect of uncertainty for entities; obviously it applies to organizations too.

Chapter 14

Commandments for the Outside

For our third set of commandments we choose those entities who are just "outside" the organization, i.e. the symbiotes. They exist in the margins of a specific organization, and are separated from members by a real boundary which may be sometimes quite arbitrary. They would like to belong, but do not. Their existence depends upon the organization they tag along with.

These are the large number of bacteria who accompany every multi-cellular organism. These are the adjuncts slogging away hoping for a shot at the tenured life. These are the ghost writers and the session musicians who live just outside the spotlight knowing that their services are essential to the organization to survive, even though the organization is blissfully ignorant of it.

These entities perceive the world from a unique perspective. They are intensely aware of the inside, of the good citizens, as well as of the outside, the wild world that exists out-of-system. However, they inhabit neither.

While we are writing these as commandments, these are not as strong or as certain as the two groups we have written for entities inside the organization. Entities in the margins of an organization have a much greater degree of choice- they can choose how "far" to be from the target organization. They can occupy a point anywhere along the continuum of an almost-member to an almost-pathogen. Thus, the range of norms or rules is also correspondingly large.

Here we will present some quasi-commandments directed towards an entity who resides on the almost-member side of the spectrum. In the next section we will look at similar words for the entity much further away.

14.1 A Non-Member will Support her Host

A non-member entity who locates herself close to an organization of member-entities probably chooses to be there because of an unfulfilled desire to belong[1].

There is a great range of entity forms and functions in this group. They may come from almost inside the organization, by the process of being just outside the arbitrary boundaries created at the point of conception of the organization. Or, they may come from far away, attracted by the central principle of the organization, but can only come so far since they started from so far away.

An entity in this position must support her host. She provides this support physically, by being a buffer from the outside. She provides this support functionally, by taking up smaller undesirable tasks that the members cannot or will not do. She provides this support emotionally, by surrounding the almost-outside members with a validation of the desirability of their membership to the organization.

In the absence of non-member supportive entities the organization itself will gradually wither and may eventually die. With the natural attrition of members, there has to be a store of willing members to draw from to replenish the organization. This replenishment may happen at different rates based on the uniformity of members in the organization.

---

[1]This need not be so- an entity can land up here by accident or by the actions of others. That situation is transient- either the other non-members detect this lack of commitment and address this risk, or the entity herself adapts and embraces the ideology of these near non-members.

14.2 A Non-Member will Crave Membership

What makes a non-member make a home at a particular distance from the boundaries of the organization? There has to be a balance of forces that pull the entity inwards toward the organization with the forces that push the entity away.

The forces that push the non-member away from the organization are clear enough. These may be too large a difference in the physical form of the non-member, or too large a difference in the compliance of the non-member to the rules of the organization.

What pulls the non-member towards the organization, then? One of the main factors is likely the attraction for the organization, i.e. an admiration of the principles of the organization in the mind of the non-member. This must be strong enough to overpower the lack of membership. The non-member gets none of the benefits of membership. In particular the non-member does not get to reduce the risk of death that the organization represents.

If anything, the non-member loves the organization more than many of the members of the organization. Her love for the organization has to be strong enough to overcome the organization's explicit denial of her desire for membership.

14.3 A Non-Member May Rescue (a few) Members

Once in a while a member falls off the organization. Perhaps he stops believing in the principles of the organization. Perhaps he gets disillusioned by the lack of responsiveness of the organization to demands for change. Perhaps he has questions the organization cannot or will not answer. In spite of his relative ignorance of the "outside" he decides to leave. This ignorance prevents him from going very far from the organization. He cannot return any more, for very few are able to join the organization. Yet he does not have all the skills needed to live independently, since the organization probably did much more for him than he was aware of. At this point the sympathetic non-member may come to his rescue.

In another context, one day the organization dies since it too is mortal. At this time there are a large number of members of various degrees of membership who are suddenly left adrift, since critical parts of the functionality of the organization are now absent.

Not all of these marooned members can be rescued. One would expect that the deeper in the organization the member was, the less likely it is that he will be able to manage the transition to independence. How does the non-member help the past member? She may show him how to survive by teaching him how to do the tasks he had previously taken for granted. She may do these tasks for him and thus carry the burden herself.

If the circumstances align, and the non-member and the past member have complementary abilities, this may be the core around which a new organization may start, with the inclusion of more non-members and past members. A new paradigm, a new day.

Chapter 15

Commandments for the Far Away

Finally, we come to the vast badlands where there are many entities, but no organizations. There is no enduring trust, and every transaction is entered in with no expectations for morality or rules. There are no rules, and there are no rule-breakers. Perhaps this was so at the beginning of the universe (from the point of view of the entities), or perhaps there is something "in the water" that prevents the formation of organizations.

Far away, perhaps beyond the visible horizon, there exist organizations. The entities may have heard of them, or may know of them. But they are either unable, or unwilling to form an organization themselves.

If you are such an entity, what should you do? What are the directives we can uncover which will help you?

Forces are at such a balance here that probably organizations cannot rise at this time. Perhaps the forces will worsen to a point where even the few entities in these badlands will break up into lower level entities. On the other hand, perhaps they will improve to allow a larger population and a convergence to the next level of organization.

If the commandments for non-member symbiotic entities have a large range, the rules for entities far away are probably not commandments at all. These are more in the form of aspirations.

Every non-member has to choose where to reside, in terms of her distance from existing organizations. We saw this in the previous section, where non-members may choose to live close to an existing organization. On the other hand, sometimes none of the existing organizations are attractive.

15.1   An Entity must Survive

Far far away from the civilization of peers one cannot live a trusting life, or assume that any of the other entities one meets will be decent and well-behaved, or that if the occasional entity is not well-behaved, then there is an infrastructure to punish these transgressors. In such cases the entity has to have the means to ensure its own survival.

The entity must be able to survive on its own, by growing or foraging for its own needs. It must be able to save functional items for a rainy day when the pickings are not as bountiful. It must monitor its environment and see if providing for its own livelihood is becoming more difficult, and hence weigh the costs and benefits of moving to a better location.

The entity must also be able to survive the occasional encounter with a similar entity. There may be benefits to such an interaction, but there are always risks. Opportunists may be monitoring her in order to steal or attack when the entity is resting or sick. There may be times when she must run away, rather than directly confront an obvious adversary.

Thus, the overriding concern is to survive, and to handle these various risks from nature and others all by herself.

15.2   An Entity may Follow No Rules

While this may sound obvious, it bears repeating. An entity far from other organizations should follow no rules.

There are many situations where it seems that there are entities which do not follow rules. Gangsters, thieves and other people far outside the rule of law may seem to follow no rules. However, most of them follow a very exact code of behavior simply in order to maintain peace. Most of the popular stories focus on the violence which happens when this order breaks down, or when there is a leadership transition. That is an unfortunate consequence of the volatility of a system driven by norms rather than rules. When they follow a set of rules, gangsters and thieves follow them far more meticulously than the average citizen. The risks of breaking these rules are far more dangerous for them.

Thus, to find a context "far far away", there must be no organizations nearby at all. It is rather unglamorous. A hardscrabble life in the middle of nowhere, where the pickings are barely enough to sustain a few hardy entities.

An entity far away from all organizations follows no rules. On the other hand, she breaks no rules. There are no rules.

15.3 An Entity may Bring Her Peers Together

While the entity far from organizations may continue the asocial life, the context may change. In some cases the environment becomes harder and the final outcome is the end of the aloof entity. On the other hand, sometimes things change for the better too. The environment becomes more favorable. More entities come to existence or move in. The neighborhood gets crowded.

At this point in the progression there are two main paths open to the entity. The first is to continue to refuse to join any group. If she persists in this choice then all around her entities may start coalescing into organizations, and finally the neighborhood will be overrun with rules. She will then either have to move to a remote location to get away, or will have to change her role to live near one or more organizations.

The other path is to lead the way to start an organization herself. She will have to formulate a value proposition for entities and draft a set of guiding principles around which other entities can agree to form an organization. She will have to lead the change.

Either way, the old way will be gone for good in this neighborhood.

Chapter 16

Multi-Human Organizations

To illustrate some of the insights from this framework in this chapter let us consider humans in a multi-layered world[1]. Humans live in many different organizations. These are the physical and social networks where we spend most of our lives and spend most of our efforts to gain membership into. Such networks arise from universities, corporations, neighborhood groups and political parties, movements and in many cases nations.

Many of these are long-standing institutions, often spanning multiple human generations. Companies like IBM and Boeing, political parties like the Democratic and Republican parties in the US, religions like Buddhism and Islam- all have existed for many human lifetimes. Many similar organizations have risen in our own lifetimes- successful startup companies like Google and Tesla, new political parties like the Libertarian and Green parties and new religious movements like ISKCON and Scientology.

Superficially they all look different, motivating their members by different inducements (including money and heaven), exhorting them to different tasks (for example making more profits or serving underprivileged communities), and trying to grow in a competitive market (by advertising their products, or by proselytizing new members).

They are also very similar in many ways. While the specific

---

[1]This example is not intended to illustrate every point mentioned in the earlier chapters, but only to provide a preview.

names may differ, they all operate in different parts of the world and have a hierarchical leadership structure. They have members or customers who associate with them for a variety of reasons, from consumer utility to brand identification to morality and faith.

Additionally, they all have to address issues at three levels described in this framework. They have to figure out how they will work with

- the level "below" them, i.e. humans or small groups of humans, which are the entities which are a part of these organizations,

- the level at which they are, i.e. other similar firms, religious movements or nations, which are the entities they compete with for their constituent members and

- the level "above" them, i.e. any confederation or trade group created of members like themselves.

The health and lifetime of each multi-human organization depends upon how well they address issues that arise from these three levels[2]. In every level there are predators, scavengers and other types of organizations that have to be considered, if possible. In this chapter we will discuss these three levels and a few other topics.

This section may be helpful for the apex leaders of multi-human organizations.

16.1 Do you know your Humans and their Motivations?

For a multi-human organization, the constituent parts are human. Thus, the critical question is why should humans join you or continue to be a part of the MHO. An equally important question

---

[2]This is within the context of a "natural" lifetime for any organization, as described in Chapter 8.

to understand is how a human's behavior changes when they join the MHO.

Unlike atoms joining a molecule, or even molecules joining together to form a virus or cell, there is far greater diversity among humans. There is also agency and free will among humans. Humans are quite capable of understanding their own choices, and learning from the consequences of choices they see other humans make. This can makes planning for human behavior in membership and motivations a never-ending game of second-guessing, finding loopholes and other trickery. But in most cases, it need not be so.

The most robust and scalable MHOs have a relatively simple and consistent allure for humans. Many are geared towards exploiting greed and/or fear, the original primal motivators. "Buy our phone and be more creative." "Join our company and make a difference to the environment." "Enroll your child at our college and let them fulfill their potential." "Use our proven methods and become a millionaire while working from home." And so on.

There are additionally two wrinkles to this scheme. The first has to do with the natural life-cycle of a human. The second has to do with human agency in joining an MHO.

16.1.1   Human Motivators

A human is motivated by different things during different phases of life. In certain phases it may be reproduction. Perhaps it is social involvement in communities. Perhaps it is money and fame as an enabler for reproduction or social standing. Perhaps it is rearing progeny. The relative importance of these motivations changes over a human lifetime.

These motivations lend themselves naturally to the formation of MHOs. There are clothes retailers who focus on teen styles, and have to be pretty nimble to keep up with the trends (perhaps even try to set them based on advertising and influence associations), and must avoid the risk of becoming "associated" with older teens. There are school improvement teams comprising of parents who devote a lot of their time to improving the educational and social environment for their own kids and for other kids.

An MHO may choose to focus narrowly on one human motivator, or may try to decide if it will address multiple motivators. A single motivator offers simplicity of mission and purpose, and can often be very scalable. Multiple motivators may sometimes offer some stability and a hedge against member churn.

Any MHO has to contend with the natural span of human membership, and has to monitor new memberships and balance that against departing members. For humans, some memberships are easier to renounce than others. A single-motivator MHO may be abandoned as soon as the human enters a new phase of life. Leaving a multi-motivator MHO may involve a more complex calculation involving benefits from a subset of motivators and the cost of contributing to the MHO overhead caused by multiple motivators. An "umbrella" MHO, like nationality or religious persuasion, can be the most difficult to give up. In many cases there are equally compelling competing MHO nations or religions, often allowing for a seamless transition. Many churches have similar organizations and at least functionally, it is easy to slip into similar roles and activities. However, for the humans, their social capital may not transfer that easily- friendships, leadership positions, and other intangible aspects.

Each human is usually a member of multiple MHOs. For example, a human may be a citizen of a nation, a follower of an established religion, a participant in the local book club, an alumnus of two universities, and a member of a worldwide family clan. This is in addition to working for a company (which may be headquartered in a different nation), and belonging to a guild of professionals. In the (idealized) past these MHOs themselves belonged to each other. Perhaps a religion was the largest group, and nation-states came under them, towns under the nation, guilds belonged to the town, families belonged to the guild, and the human belonged to the family. There was, in effect, no membership conflict (or perhaps complete membership conflict- abandon one, and you have to abandon many others).

Today, there is ample scope for conflict. Humans may work for the same company, but be of different religions and of different nations. In a connected society geography has been removed as a qualifying attribute for belonging to MHOs. This allows much more inter-MHO mobility for humans in order to achieve their personal goals. On the other hand, it also needs more inclusivity and socialization in order to reduce conflict. That may also mean coming up with a unique set of behavior or adoptable attributes in order to signal belonging- a dress code (whether it is tattoos and beards, or suits and ties) or a set of behaviors (attending off-sites and socials, or writing research papers).

16.1.2 Membership at Birth

In "umbrella" MHOs, and in many multi-generational MHOs, many members come into the MHO at birth[3]. Nations, religions and many geographically-based MHOs commonly allow this method of membership.

For such members there is no intrinsic motivation or understanding of the nature of their own membership. While membership-at-birth allows an MHO to grow "organically", it may risk dilution of the collective motivation.

Thus, an umbrella MHO has to devote significant resources into socializing foundlings into its concept and founding principles to complement the social bonds formed with other members of the organization. The methods by which this is done is reasonably evident for nations and religions- some form of regular school hours devoted to the history and philosophy of the organization.

Other MHOs also use schooling/socialization in ways which overlap our earlier exploration of the roles of functional activities and artistic activities[4]. Universities use sports teams as both competition against other universities, and as socialization for their undergraduate students. Many successful corporations use mis-

---

[3]This idea can be extended to affiliation membership, where a member brings in other members into the MHO primarily because of their human affiliation rather than due to motivations aligned with the organization's reason for existence.

[4]See Chapter 5 on competition and art.

sion statements and off-site activities to achieve the same goals[5].

Beyond that it is often very competitive. Companies actively recruit their competitor's employees. Universities court students from all parts of their state, country and internationally. Nations compete as well, increasing the individual and collective mobility of humans. With increasing scrutiny of many aspects of these MHOs, there is greater volatility in MHO memberships compared to a few decades ago. This increases the need to have a simple and transparent motivational mission, which is a very difficult thing. The increasing numbers of new members in an MHO may also create conflict with existing and birthright members.

16.2 Who are your MHO Friends and Enemies?

No organization exists in a vacuum, particularly since humans have been social for millennia. Thus, there are all varieties of multi-human organizations, and they coexist and compete for humans. In addition, they also compete among themselves. We can illustrate these competitions by drawing analogies with the biological kingdoms and ecosystems that have been extensively studied.

First, there are those MHOs that are the most similar to your MHO. If you run delivery services, then there are other delivery services which may operate in the same city and other cities. You compete with them for humans to work for you, as well as for customers, who are humans and other organizations who need your services. When humans move from other cities and countries they may come to you and your competitor MHOs for jobs (and membership). Thus, any given MHO is connected to many MHOs as part of a supply chain or a value chain ("vertical" connections), and to other MHOs identical to themselves which provide the same service in this value chain ("horizontal" connections).

---

[5]When done properly this works well. When done poorly this lands up in dysfunctionality cartoons and streaming episodes.

There are also other kinds of MHOs, more akin to predators and scavengers. There are other firms who may offer to buy up your company, equivalent to members of a food chain- cows eating grass, and tigers eating cows. After buying an MHO the predator may integrate it into their own operations with minor changes, or may break it up into pieces to "digest" the pieces of value and discard the scraps. For example, many startups have an explicit "exit plan" based on the presence of larger predator MHOs[6]. In the 1980s many companies had a thriving business of buying older conglomerates and selling the pieces more profitably.

Thus your MHO competitive strategy is quite similar to competitive strategies in an ecosystem, and depend upon what your MHO is equivalent to- are you a tree, a zebra or a wolf? That is, are you a primary value creator, a value extractor, or an apex predator? Perhaps your "natural" death comes from being consumed, and perhaps your natural death comes from fighting others like you. Or perhaps your "natural" death comes from microbes and system breakdown, completing the circle of life.

16.3   When do we Collaborate with other MHOs?

16.3.1   MHOs Locked in Stalemate

While there is always a first business in any given industry for a product or service, we have observed that such a situation does not last very long. Very soon there many similar MHOs in the environment/industry competing vigorously for a share of the fast shrinking untapped business potential. After that, unfortunately, it slowly turns into a bloodbath.

A bloodbath between MHOs can mean different things for humans. It may mean an increasing number of job changes, both involuntary and voluntary. A more likely outcome is loss of jobs

---

[6]Some companies which serve the role of predator MHOs in this context can be the networking company Cisco, and social networking and search giants like Facebook and Google.

and livelihood, with little transferability of previously acquired skills. If the humans work in symbiotic roles to a specific MHO, then they are slightly more likely to transfer their roles to any other MHO.

This provides a great incentive to collaborate and reduce the immediate chances of such a bloodbath, at least among those MHOs which collaborate. Thus, in a very competitive context it is imperative that you guide your MHO to collaborate with others. Collaboration may take different forms. It may be showing an unwillingness to invade each other's turf. It may be setting up an annual meeting in the form of an industry conference. The pricing of your products and services may signal your desire to not compete too intensively. Your advertising campaign may signal a similar desire to collaborate implicitly.

None of this signaling will amount to much unless you have first established that you can fight to the end[7], or are at least locked in strategic stalemate.

16.3.2 Existing Federations of MHOs

There may already exist a confederation of similar MHOs who may want you to join their super-MHO. These may be associations and industry trade groups. These are the next level, and are created by MHOs from the same risk-aversion that all organizations and entities share. They provide a venue for MHOs to be collegial, to coordinate their operations and strategies, and to address common threats together.

In some countries the primary form of business is a large conglomerate of related and unrelated businesses linked by cross-ownership. Sometimes these are supply chains which are interacting parts of a value chain, and cross-ownership[8] allows them to share information and align their development plans around new products and services.

Japanese conglomerates known as keiretsu (e.g. Mitsui and Sumitomo), and Korean ones known as chaebol (e.g. Samsung

---

[7]A very preliminary set of guidelines are listed in Chapter 15.
[8]This may mean that your main buyer owns 20% of your company.

and Hyundai) are examples of these. These evolved organically in order to prevent takeover attempts and to help their member companies weather economic downturns without going bankrupt. In many cases these conglomerates are held together by a central financial institution. On a similar note, many startups often belong to the ecosystem created by their early investors, and are often able to grow with the support of these ecosystems.

Is an existing confederation of MHOs the right one to join for you? That may depend upon many factors, including how late you are to the "game", and what your role will be. There is often enough benefit to justify being a symbiote MHO- an organization which does important jobs that the core members of the federation will not (or cannot) do.

16.4   (MHO) Stability from (Human) Instability

16.4.1   An MHO's Nervous/Operating System

Unlike biological systems in animals, all MHOs have to withstand a blistering pace of change in the very foundational elements of their organization. For example, the basic biochemistry of cells and the basic signaling mechanisms in the animal nervous system have probably been unchanged for many millions of years. However, for the last five hundred years the basis of communications and operations in MHOs have changed radically.

In the past human lifetime humans have gone from using expensive community telegraphs and household telephones to using much less expensive personal mobile devices for communication. In addition our memories and processing capabilities have also been augmented from using solely our brains and notebooks to the same class of personal devices.

This has tremendous consequence for MHO operating design. These implications are the most visible in the structure of businesses founded in the last decade or two, compared to those founded earlier. Thus, MHOs founded earlier have the constant challenge of having to change their internal operating principles as the underlying "biochemistry" of communication and transportation changes over time.

Fortunately, in many parts of the world there exist robust networks of consulting and information technology organizations (who are MHOs themselves) who have made it their mission to help these older MHOs upgrade their operating technologies. Often the promise is greater than the execution of the transition. Ironically, this relationship can itself be the basis of a super-MHO.

16.4.2   Leadership Transition in an MHO

After you (a human) have gained control of the running of your MHO, it is perhaps legitimate to enjoy (for a short while) the benefits that come from this accomplishment. There will be enough fawning members to use an association with you as their pathway to power and status. There will be enough members to give you willingly what previously you had to fight for- money, objects or companionship. (On the other hand, there will also be scheming courtiers who patiently wait for you to make unrecoverable mistakes). After you have satisfied these primary urges, you may face a long tenure of guiding your MHO to success.

Yet at some time you have to wonder what will happen after you are gone. How will the MHO survive? Who will succeed you? Will it be one of your team? Will it be an unknown plucked from the villages of your kingdom? Will it be your own child? Are you so attached to your progeny (biological or operational) that you overlook their shortcomings and set up a system where they will be the leaders after you?

Leadership transition is the challenge with all historical monarchies, as well as modern dictatorships. It is also the problem with large corporations, as well as coaching staff of prominent sports teams. At times the transition is disorderly, risking a breakup of the MHO. At other times it looks orderly, but is achieved at the expense of weakening the organization and planting the seeds of its demise.

For the MHO to be sustainable beyond you, there has to be

conflict within it, and some system of choosing the next leader from that conflict. There has to be a method of grooming leaders from the common members, with a gradual increase of responsibilities and power as well as the possibility of entering anywhere in the hierarchy. Each step may be achieved after competition[9]. This method has to be independent of the current leader . Executed improperly, it may lead to a palace cabal which installs puppet leaders[10].

This is, necessarily, chaotic and unstable. It often tempts leaders to set up an orderly system so that every decision and every step appears to be unanimous and collaborative. "Troublemakers" are often ejected from leadership roles (and also from the MHO itself, which may lead them to form competing MHOs).

Grooming leaders is another area in which MHOs collaborate. Leaders are groomed, and then sent out to other MHOs when opportunities arise. This gives them an opportunity to prove their skills in other contexts, and allows for an external validation of their capabilities, albeit tinged with fortunate circumstances. However, in a competitive sense, it also results in a uniformity of operating strategies across MHOs since there is a sharing of "best practices" and competitive "bench marking".

The ability of umbrella MHOs like nations and religions in socializing infants into membership has often led to a stability in organizational leadership and leadership structures. This often weakens them in the long run, and lacking a leader who can break up the status quo, can often lead to their glide into obscurity.

There is no easy answer. Perhaps the only answer is that all that comes into existence must also go out of existence. All leaders can do is to ensure continuity of their mission across MHOs.

---

[9]This may be different from the artistic competitions between members that we have mentioned in the framework (See Chapter 5).

[10]For example, an institution like the Praetorian Guard in ancient Rome which effectively controlled the leadership position.

16.4.3 Nurturing Thieves and Scoundrels in an MHO

The problems created by the push to make an MHO crime-free are not obvious, unlike the transition difficulties of leadership change in MHOs[11].

Moving towards an MHO where there are no thieves and scoundrels requires creating a group in which there is strong adherence to rules and norms. While this sounds great for those inside the MHO, it is unfortunately not that nice for those who are at the edges and have to interact with other MHOs and other independent humans. Assuming that external MHOs and humans follow slightly different rules and norms, it becomes difficult for the home MHO humans to interact with them.

Complete uniformity of member behavior is unstable since it allows for no way of addressing any changes in the internal or external environment. Over time it leads to an increasing separation from the environment in which the MHO was created. When this distance becomes too large and the MHO breaks down, the humans who were part of the MHO will probably also be completely unfit for the external environment, and effectively die as well.

Having rule breakers in the MHO makes the MHO more robust[12]. Among other benefits, it keeps regular members aware of the existence of rule-breakers, and it justifies the existence of a police force which stays in shape and directs its attention to legitimate targets.

---

[11]These problems are quite well documented- in history for nations and religions, and in the business press and research for businesses and community organizations.

[12]See Section 6.2 for a discussion on rule breaking and its organizational benefits.

Chapter 17

Singularity, or the Next Level

17.1 The Mirage of Technological Singularity

The most common popular use of singularity is the technology singularity, described first by John von Neumann. Today the term describes runaway computing and artificial intelligence that self-upgrades until it breaks free of its human minders. In short, perhaps a modern retelling of the tale of Frankenstein's creature.

Technological singularity is a bogeyman that we all love to feel scared of (or alternately, a Utopian overlordship we should all welcome). It is nowhere nearby.

Machine intelligence and AI do not exist independent of humans. Today (I write this in 2020) they exist as a reasonably fragile layer on top of robust human networks delivering electricity, air-conditioning, silicon, hand-curated data, and armies of programmers. It is not Watson which defeated Ken Jennings in Jeopardy; it was IBM and its team of human programmers working with tons of computing power. It is not the Tesla electric car that drives itself; it is the Tesla company of engineers, factory workers and programmers who make "autonomous" driving possible. Add to that the additional infrastructure of legal property rights and functioning capital markets that enable the "greed" for a successful initial public offering (IPO) of company shares, as well as the organizational structure of the specific companies and the management expertise it represents.

As an analogy, machine intelligence is as close to breaking out from its human masters as solar panels are to becoming self repairing and replicating (like trees, which do the similar task of capturing the sun's solar energy into another form of energy). Which is to say, it is rather far off.

Yet, there has been real change- a different form of singularity. The policy responses to COVID-19 during 2020 clearly show the change.

17.2   Organizational Singularity

When did a cell realize that it was no longer an independent entity, and belonged to a multi-cellular organism?

If we can answer this question, we will know whether a singularity has already happened for us as well. Before we start, let us spend some time to consider the exact type of singularity we are discussing.

What happens when an entity becomes a part of a higher level entity for the first time? Does its behavior change? I would conjecture not.

When a water molecule becomes part of a cell, it does not change its chemical behavior. When a salt molecule in the body is recruited to work in a nerve cell, it does not change its nature. It behaves as it has always done. The change in a molecule or atom's environment, of course, does not usually happen suddenly (unless we inject saline into a human body, but let us not get distracted). It happens gradually. Not that the atom cares.

When a cell becomes a part of a multi-cellular organism, this change happens over many generations. Perhaps the start of the process happens when cells multiply and create a colony that ends up regulating the local water chemistry. Perhaps over time DNA kinship becomes more important over generations, driven by evolution to consider collaborations that help the colony survive. To a member of each successive generation there is nothing unusual in its life or environment, nothing changes drastically.

Humans have changed their environment quite drastically in the past century- the chemical environment of air and water, the biological environment of the foods consumed and the informational environment of communication and technology. Each successive cohort of human children adapts better to the environment they are born in when compared to how their parents fare (for whom the environment has changed since their own childhood). Over the last hundred years the changes compared across two generations are nothing less than magic, yet most of us seem to take it in our stride.

How deep are we in the formation of the next level? Did it start from the code of Hammurabi, the laws of Manu and the rules created by the Zhou dynasty? Did it start from the creation of the bureaucracy framework in France, or from the first statues in the US recognizing corporations as legally equivalent to humans and covered by the same protections given to humans by the constitution? Did it start from the first email sent on the ARPA network in the early 1970s? Or was it the iPhone in 2007?

Each of these groups of laws or technology form a community whose basis is different from the physical, chemical or biochemical kinship that was common before it. As many have pointed out, the advent of these different modes of belonging have been accelerating in recent decades.

These codes and technologies form the basis of "organizational singularity" for humans; each of these have helped take one more step towards the next level of organization. How far are we into the process, and how can we know?

17.3   Visible Consequences of Organizational Singularity

Each step that we humans take towards the emergence of a "new" layer has consequences for our activities. This may look like the steady march of progress, or science, or religion through history. In the moment, however, it proceeds in fits and starts. What may seem like a great improvement will not last unless it provides the individuals or organizations a significant survival advantage. What constitutes an advantage (or disadvantage) may not be visible to humans in their own lifetimes. Thus, it is rather difficult to identify the moment at which the next layer emerged, or will emerge. The only reason we are able to do this is because the progress of emergence of the organization is happening far faster for us than for previous layers, and also because we keep records of history.

The various worldwide reactions to the coronavirus in 2020 affords us a rare instance of evaluating where we stand with regard to organizational singularity. It allows us to evaluate how far we humans are in the process of being folded into the next layer. It is showing us how robust our various systems of business, religion, government, or other forms are. Historically there have been worse epidemics, far worse. While it is difficult to look back and reconstruct how the human population reacted to each pandemic, it would not be unreasonable to say that the reaction in 2020 was unusual.

While this is specific to the reactions to coronavirus, this should be applied to every large adverse incident (hopefully there won't be too many of them in each lifetime).

17.3.1 Instantaneous Information Diffusion

The rate at which information is conveyed to a significant portion (say 20%) of the human population is unprecedented, and can be measured in seconds. It is limited only by which social network we belong to, and how frequently we are willing to check our phone apps.

Every communication technology has been considered with wonder. The telegraph and the telephone were wonderful inventions. However, they required human socialization to complete the last leg- we had to talk to our friends and neighbors.

In some ways the digitally native generations that are growing up with phones and wearables are almost like neurons, collecting information across all their feeds and choosing to propagate some to their own network of friends by the simple actions of liking and sharing. While this is enabled by the algorithms and servers of the specific social networks, information frequently jumps from network to network. This propagation of unattributed information across such large portions of humanity are unprecedented.

During the coronavirus epidemic this information propagation mechanism was capable of drowning out the controlled methods traditionally used to drive population behavior. It is in fact tempting to consider this the first example of entire nations catching the flu and going to bed with fever. This happened even in developing countries where the consequences of "going to bed with a fever" are devastating to poorer sections of the population with no social safety net.

17.3.2 Faster Action after an Incident

There is also a critical mass to each real-time reaction to an event. The increased intensity of communication coalesces each group with similar opinions. The arguments (or flames) also play out in real time, and the policy-making apparatus also participates in the game, making the incident-reaction-action cycle a matter of days, instead of months.

Ironically, these networks often transcends national boundaries, making it difficult to separate the initial incident and the resultant policy changes. As a consequence, in the competitive market between nations, the fast reaction cycle of some nations forces others to react even if their citizens did not initiate the reaction.

This has been clear during the coronavirus times in many areas, from the pressure to develop vaccines, to social distancing norms (even if wildly inappropriate to the context), to monetary stimulus packages to prevent wholesale economic meltdown, and other areas. Differences in opinion between those who wanted to extend the lock-down and those who want to open up also play out in hours and days.

187

17.4 The Singularity Today

Ironically, the technologies in the very near future will render these amazing incidents quite boring. It is worthwhile remembering that the older generation can remember a time when an entire neighborhood shared a single wired telephone line, and that seemed a wonder in itself. Some of us remember a time when mass media reached most homes in a country and opened up an entire world to the family, broadcasting world shaking events, presidential speeches and daily reports from war zones. We remember a time when a single music band could have the entire world listening to them in the form of grooved vinyl discs.

Each of these past events seemed to be miraculous when they happened, and also generated considerable debate. Are we forgetting how to remember, now that we can print books? Are we forgetting how to multiply, now that we have calculators? Are we diminishing "real" friendships, now that we are "friends" with a few thousand entities on a social network?

Today's tools of social media and wearables will also become obsolete in a decade, or perhaps less. This, now, is an outcome of current technology, and as technology evolves, new tools will evolve to keep pace with it.

Organizational and social singularity is intimately linked to technology- technological singularity has always been subsumed into organizational singularity. In the history of the earth these "technological" innovations have been in the fields of chemistry, biochemistry, macro-molecules and so on- mirroring the layers of organization as we have identified them. Each one is driven by competition and overcrowding, initially giving it's adopters a way out of extreme competition and assure its members a little more reassurance of survival. The next singularity will do something similar- give humans a little more assurance of stability and protection from the wide world outside.

Many of us will be alive to see these changes, and may even forget to be amazed by them. The novelty of this too shall pass, and we shall not remember.

Chapter 18

Epilogue

18.1 Next...

What can we do with this framework? Does it allow us to predict the outcome of a specific business or organizational conflict? Does it allow us to predict the consequences of some new kind of communication or transportation technology? Does it allow us to invest in specific social movements or entrepreneurial startups?

That may depend upon not just this framework, but also intimate familiarity with the context in which a specific future-gazing question is framed. There is also a qualitative difference between reality and these questions and answers (similar to the difference between the beauty of a sunset and physics-based explanations involving wavelengths of light and light scattering in the earth's atmosphere).

Technology, competition and innovation will continue to provide new tools that will allow new organizations to be more efficient at the same size, or grow larger in number or reach. This has been the story of human and organizational evolution over the past few millennia. Thus, at our level of abstraction future organizations will look very similar to current organizations.

Having said that, it will still be quite entertaining to let our imaginations free to roam within the constraints of this framework. We call them constraints, but a framework which allows for everything under the sun (and many things over it as well) is hopefully vast enough to accommodate many things we can imagine.

It is important to acknowledge that they are still constraints, since many of the future-gazing narratives that are popular today do violate this framework. No matter how desirous we may be of a Lennon-esque "Imagine" future, we don't see any potential for a completely competition-free universe. A competition-free and peaceful part of the universe? Sure- look no further than inside your own body, where billions of cells live in peace and harmony (mostly). But right outside there are viruses, bacteria, mosquitoes, the man with a knife in the dark alley, and other countries looking to stiff each other on trade deals.

If we have to work through the consequences of any technology on the social and economic structure of human social groups, then we have to start from the basic principles from this framework. There will be competition, there will be multiple competing entities and organizations, and there will always be outsiders who are not part of any organization (and so on). In the absence of competitive pressure, the single entity or firm will increasingly be out of touch with evolving technologies and behavior until finally it fails.

Each new technology will have consequences in terms of how organizations based on those tools would look or behave. Old-tech organizations will have to figure out ways to adapt while they use their scale to stave off the upcoming upheaval.

These elements interact in many more ways than we can imagine. Thus we really cannot predict the pace at which any competition or self-organizing will occur. In a fundamental mathematical sense, it is not only chaotic, it is post-chaotic (which means that intelligent agents consciously structure parts of their world so that "inside" there is stability instead of chaos). Ironically, post-chaotic often looks simpler than chaos.

Any competitive prediction for a set of entities must also consider the stability and nature of competition in the layers above it, and in the layers below it.

I have debated trying to tease out the implications of this framework for various parts of our universe and the layers it is organized into. It is easy to see that I really do not have the expertise for this next task. Further words from me will expose even more my inadequate preparation. Thus further analysis will have to wait for future collaborations, and for others to take forward.

18.2 Cynicism and Action

Some readers have pointed out that this take on the world and organizations is extremely cynical, and that this is a very negative way of framing life. Irrespective of what you feel about this view, I encourage you to read on.

The purpose of any worldview or framework is to provide a guide for our immediate actions. As an example, the sum of knowledge a poker player has- of odds, probabilities, player styles, game theory and everything else, works to express itself in very simple actions at each point of time- to raise, call or to fold. Similarly, our views on how we work, how society works, and how people work, as well as the sum total of all our beliefs work together to inform us of what we should do in the next moment, the next time we meet a stranger on the street, or the next time we take our kid to school.

Cynicism is an individual's state of mind when she has lost her previous guiding frameworks and has not yet found the next one. Do we stop acting when we do not have principles to guide us? Of course not. There is inertia, or muscle memory, or whatever we wish to call it. We continue breathing, we continue eating and brushing our teeth, and we continue to smile and greet strangers on the street in small towns. These do not require frameworks and thoughts. These are habits and life necessities.

When a person's worldview has been completely shattered, they still continue living on the basis of habits. For example, upon the first post-adolescent encounter with the death of a loved one, one continues living, even though one may have given up the central concept of a benevolent God. Yet even in this state of inertia the mind works furiously to make sense of it all. We want to believe, and often we work ourselves into a state where we rework our previous beliefs so that they incorporate this new contradiction. If we cannot, then we start the long process of constructing a new belief system.

To some it may seem that I am cynical due to my belief in this framework, since many of its elements appear to be in direct contradiction to their core beliefs. I am most definitely not a cynic. What I have laid out is the current basis for my actions, since I do believe that any worldview must be as consistent as possible with as wide a known set of facts about the physical world. Ironically, this has taken me till middle-age to figure out, so the majority of my past decisions were not guided by it. But now that I believe in this framework, I do use it to guide my actions.

Coupled with my middle-age view of human development of both boys/men and girls/women, I also believe that each age has its own appropriate worldview and framework for action. There is no value in trying to show the twenty-year old human the consequences of sexual attraction that they are feeling and interpreting as love. In fact, it would be really counterproductive to try (or worse, to succeed) to get them to adopt a transcendental worldview where love is a powerful illusion driven by the reptilian part of our brains.

The purpose of this framework, then, is to drive action when each of us is all grown up, and has delivered on our human and social responsibilities. A significant part of those social responsibilities may have included nurturing kids, going to war for our beliefs and our clan, and competing fiercely against our peers to win as high a prize as we can, and as many times as we can.

When all is done, including socializing our offspring into these same age-appropriate values, it is time to think broader and ask how we can design systems that will allow as many of us to thrive as possible. How do we design systems that are robust, self-correcting, and sustainable? This is our role, since we humans have moved on from the "blind" forces of physics, chemistry, biochemistry and natural evolution. We now design and operate systems as large as companies, religions/movements and economies. Unlike natural biological evolution, we tweak these systems every month and every year, each time we uncover a potential weakness.

Thus, we need the most robust frameworks possible to guide us, and the longest time horizon that we can possibly comprehend. That is the motivation behind this book.

Have you delivered your family responsibilities, and ensured your offspring a reasonable life ahead? Then you need to expand out of the values and frameworks that drove your actions for the previous two decades, and figure out what you must believe in next. Once you have such a goal, use this framework to create something bigger than you that will last long after you are gone.

18.3 Morality

Some readers have asked whether this framework allows for morality, or supports it. The simple answer to this question is that this supports morality, but in a stranger way than considered conventionally.

At one level, the framework points out both the triviality of many rituals enforced by our cherished human institutions (which many people, particularly youngsters have observed), as well as the greater necessity of these rituals. Our nations and religions have many rules and norms. They are trivial since they are reasonably arbitrary and can be substituted with many similar rules and norms. But they are necessary since that is the mode of identification and belonging. They are necessary for the identification of us-vs-them. While that may sound arbitrary, it is also necessary since the competition between similar organizations makes all surviving organizations better (as a collective).

If our final goal is to achieve a union of all religions and humans, or all nations and humans, then that must always remain as an unattainable aspiration. A thriving community of nations who are continuously bickering about small and big things makes the collective of nations stronger. If we ever got to a point when all (or most) unite under one banner, that can only be a transient situation till either it breaks up due to internal contradictions, or there arises a competitor union made of the members who where deemed unworthy of the first union.

The greater morality lies in realizing that it is the choice between organizations that makes members' lives better, if some degree of mobility is possible. If we ever come to a situation in the world where, say, there is only one superpower, then that superpower will have no need to evolve to make life better for its citizens. After all, what choice do they have!

Thus, the morality presented here is not an ideal morality, which promises the best world for everyone. This is a pragmatic morality which tries to stay close enough to a functioning and acceptable world for most of us, and works to decrease the numbers of those who do not have such a life yet. As an oft-repeated example (communism), forcing equality on all citizens has not made them more equal, richer, or citizen's lives more fulfilling. On the other hand (capitalism), having them compete with each other, often losing their jobs, and even allowing for the occasional unscrupulous charlatan, has made greater progress for most citizens. This system would break down as well, unless there is a competing nation, or a competing economic philosophy. Capitalism needs the threat of communism to evolve in line with the desires of its citizens. Capitalism with no opposing economic philosophy will quickly regernate communism in one or two generations.

Perhaps we are now beyond this obvious comparison between communism and capitalism. Perhaps today the active debate may be between versions of capitalism which are possible due to advances in behavioral science and technology. What better morality can we hope to have in the mortal world...

Part III

Appendices

Chapter 19

A1: The Framework

19.1 Axioms, Theorems and Others

The skeletal structure of Part I of the book, stated in axioms, theorems and other official-looking statements. These took form during 2013-2014, and the core statements were formulated in 2016.

19.1.1 In Chapter 2

Layers:

Fact 1. *The observable universe is organized in layers, presumably starting from subatomic "things", and then atoms, molecules, cells, multi-cellular animals and plants, social organizations, and more complex ones.*

19.1.2 In Chapter 3

Entities:

Definition 2. An entity is a physical or virtual thing that is separate from its environment. It has a boundary and is identifiable by its form or function. Its design may not be unique, i.e.other similar entities may exist in the same environment. It has a finite lifetime with a distinct birth and death.

Competition:

Definition 3. Symmetric competition (henceforth "competition" as evident from context) is defined as the short and long term conflict between similar entities for resources and/or replication opportunities.

Strategy:

Definition 4. A strategy is defined as a series of actions taken by an entity in order to move its environment's current configuration (or future configurations over a specific timescale) closer to one that provides the entity some resources or advantage over other entities.

19.1.3   In Chapter 4

Survival:

Proposition 5. *The most fundamental strategic objective of an entity is survival.*

Uncertainty:

Definition 6. There are three types of uncertainty that any entity faces in its environment. (1) The first type of uncertainty comes from random events influenced by almost no external factors. (2) The second type of uncertainty comes from interaction of various physical items in the environments, which leads to chaotic behavior. (3) The third type of uncertainty comes from the strategic actions of other entities at various timescales, including similar entities in the same layer.

The greatest uncertainty:

Proposition 7. *The largest source of uncertainty for an entity is the actions of entities that are the most similar to itself.*

Cooperation:

Proposition 8. *From Propositions (5) and (7), it follows that every entity can choose to compete with similar entities to keep the rewards for itself on winning, or cooperate with them in order to share the rewards from acting together.*

Achilles Choice:

Proposition 9. *An entity's may classify its long-term strategy as a choice between a short and eventful life by going alone or a long and uneventful life by cooperating with others.*

The basis of organizations:

Theorem 10. *The basis of the existence of organizations is the decision by some entities to give up freedom of choice of action, in return for a reduction in the volatility of the daily search for desirable resources, e.g. recognition, food and mates.*

Organizations:

Definition 11. An Organization is a collection of entities that have decided to adhere to certain norms of behavior and competition in a certain area of competition so that individually each one shares the gains from its own wins with others, in return for getting a share of the win of any other entity in the organization.

Symbiotes:

Proposition 12. *The existence of organizations also gives rise to the possibilities of entities that have partial membership of the organization. Symbiotes are entities who are precluded from full membership of an organization due to specific reasons but still provide value to the organization in other ways.*

Dead ends:

Corollary 13. *Symmetric competition rule breakers are a dead end. They do not create parallel organizations.*

Membership and rules:

Corollary 14. *An organization necessitates*
(a) the definition of membership and member attributes,
(b) norms/rules and principles which determine behavior and outcomes, and
(c) a monitoring overhead to ensure that members adhere to the norms/rules and principles.

19.1.4   In Chapter 5

In-system competition:

Proposition 15. *The existence of organizations does not eliminate competition. This creates a continuum of competition options for member entities, represented in the extreme as in-system competition and out-of-system competition. These are differentiated primarily by the possibility of death in course of competition (or permanent involuntary competitive elimination) .*

In-system competitive parity:

Corollary 16. *Since in-system competition necessitates engaging in competition without death,*
(a) "no death" is not credible unless the rules/norms enforce more parity than is expected, and
(b) "the competition" is not interesting unless all participants (and viewers) honor the competitive element.

Functional benefit:

Definition 17. The functional benefit associated with an item is an attribute of the item that is directly linked to survival benefits for the entity possessing the item.

In-system competition:

Corollary 18. *In-system competition by member entities*
(a) necessitates the commitment of significant resources, towards
(b) the development of capabilities with little functional benefit, in order to

(c) compete in complex competitions against other entities, with

(d) the possibility of very little functional gain (from the stated rewards), but with

(e) real rewards, that flow from the

(f) endorsement of the competition's rules by both participants and any audience members within the organization.

Art:

Definition 19. Art is defined as

(i) the creation of any object or skill

(ii) to be used in implicit or explicit in-system competitions

(iii) which requires significant investment of time and effort

(iv) but which provides no immediate functional benefit.

19.1.5   In Chapter 6

Total enforcement:

Proposition 20. *No organization can enforce total compliance to a rule.*

Voluntary compliance:

Corollary 21. *An organization depends upon voluntary compliance to rules.*

Changing rules:

Corollary 22. *To function well over time an organization must ensure that rules change to reflect the needs of both the entity and the organization, and ensure continued voluntary compliance.*

Rule followers:

Definition 23. There is a continuum of rule followers. At one extreme are habitual rule followers who do not have an understanding of the structure or purpose of rules. At the other end are conscious rule followers who have an understanding of the nature of rules and the relative importance of different rules.

Rule breakers:

Definition 24. There are two main categories of (member) rule breakers- ignorant and conscious. Within these two broad categories there are the following main types of rule breakers

(a) (Ignorant) Children: Entities born within the system who are learning the rules of the organization break rules and are forgiven even if the outcome is severe. A child's leeway in breaking rules decreases in proportion to its consequences as it grow older and stronger.

(b) (Ignorant) Visitors: Entities who are visiting the organization from other organizations may break etiquette rules and are often forgiven since they have not yet learned the many unwritten rules of the organization (or are habitually following the rules from the "home" organization).

(c) (Conscious) Marginal: Member entities push the rules to the extent that will usually not incur penalties (due to enforcement costs). Conversely, rules are often written taking into account that there will always be marginal rule breakers.

(d) (Conscious) Teenagers: Young adult entities usually break the apparently arbitrary rules as an act of rebellion when they have to choose between belonging to the organization or retaining the childhood freedom to break the rules.

(e) (Conscious) Central: Entities who belong to the system for a long time may see an inherent flaw or contradiction in the letter or intent of various rules or norms, and therefore break the system itself rather than any individual rule. They may do it for personal benefit or for organizational benefit.

Rule breakers and system evolution:

Corollary 25. *The existence of rule breakers accelerates boundary formation of a proto-organization.*

Conscious rule-breakers and strategy:

Proposition 26. *Variations in organizational strategy may occur through conscious rule-breaking by entities in the form of teenagers and central-rule-breakers.*

Good and bad:

Definition 27. Good entities follow the rules of the organization. Bad entities do not follow the rules.

Neither good not bad in absence of organizations:

Corollary 28. *There cannot be good or bad entities unless there is an organization or a system with breakable rules.*

Deeply embedded members:

Corollary 29. *The deeper an entity is embedded in the organization (as defined by the totality of the entity's membership attributes and rule-breaking history), the more absolute is its belief in the system, as well as its tendency to see other entities in absolute terms of good and bad.*

Leaders:

Corollary 30. *An an organization's leadership cannot be ignorant rule-followers. While "lower" leaders enforce rules, "middle" leaders must understand rule-breakers and the reason for the organization's existence. Finally, "upper" leaders must understand the environment external to the organization- symbiotes, other organizations and predators (see Chapter 7).*

Closing the loop:

Theorem 31. *After a successful organization has defined itself and has been imitated or has procreated to fill up the opportunity/niche, it now faces the same choice that its constituent entities faced one layer ago. Thus, successful organizations are the entities for the next layer.*

19.1.6   In Chapter 7

Scavengers:

Definition 32. Scavengers are organizations which use pieces of earlier organizations that include entities and working groups of entities. Scavengers initially form in an entity-rich environment where stable organizations have not yet formed, and continue into environments with stable organizations where they continue to reuse parts of organizations that have ceased to be organized (i.e. died).

Predators:

Definition 33. (a) Horizontal predators are organizations which use the entities of existing viable organizations. They are composed of the same entities. While prey organizations are structured on some spontaneous basis, predator organizations are structured on the premise of reusing parts of the prey.

(b) Vertical predators are entities which attack the entities of an organization in order to capture the components of the entities. Depending on the severity of the attack, the organization may also be compromised.

Predators and evolution:

Corollary 34. *Predators push both species (the prey and themselves) along one dimension of evolutionary movement. If the predator is tied in to one species of prey, they may survive and perish together.*

Symbiotes:

Definition 35. Symbiotes are entities which start off as asymmetric competitors, and then co-evolve in order to provide each other mutual benefits without causing the immediate death of either.

19.1.7 In Chapter 8

Death:

Definition 36. Death is defined as the irrevocable state of the entity/organization which prevents it from participating in any activity with its peers. This is also accompanied by a breakdown of the organization into entities. As a consequence, its entities may also die.

Corollary 37. *An organization may die due to external or internal causes External causes include*
(a) out-of-system competition and predators,
(b) lack of resources and
(c) physical accidents.
Internal causes include
(d) a failure by its constituent entities to continue cooperating and/or
(e) a subversion of the organization by free-riders, and/or
(f) programmed deterioration in order to increase population diversity,

After death:

Corollary 38. *The survival of the component entities after an organization's death depends inversely on the intensity of cooperation between the entities during the lifetime of the organization.*

Layers below:

Conjecture 39. *There exist earlier/more fundamental physical levels of entities and organization which cumulatively result in the existence of the atom as we know it.*

Layers above:

Conjecture 40. *There can exist later/more abstract social levels of entities and organizations which are built upon the human organizations (e.g. clans, tribes, religions, countries) as we know them.*

Index

www.ingramcontent.com/pod-product-compliance
Lightning Source LLC
Chambersburg PA
CBHW070805050426
42452CB00011B/1898